W9-AVT-370

Table Talk!

Table Talk!

(365 ways to reclaim the family dinner hour)

by
Steve and Ruth Bennett

BOB ADAMS, INC.
Holbrook, Massachusetts

Published by Bob Adams, Inc. 260 Center Street, Holbrook, MA 02343

ISBN: 1-55850-300-5

Printed in the United States of America

A   B   C   D   E   F   G   H   I   J

Library of Congress Cataloging-in-Publication Data

Bennett, Steve.
  Table Talk : 365 ways to reclaim the family dinner hour / by Steve and Ruth Bennett.
      p.   cm.
  ISBN 1-55850-300-5 : $6.95
  1. Communication in the family. 2. Dinners and dining. I. Bennett, Ruth (Ruth Loetterle) II. Title.
III. Title: 365 ways to reclaim the family dinner hour. IV. Title: Three hundred and sixty-five ways
to reclaim the family dinner hour.
  HQ518.B44   1993
  646.7'8—dc20   93-36846
                                                                                                  CIP

This publication is designed to provide accurate and authoritative information with regard to the subject
matter covered. It is sold with the understanding that the publisher is not engaged in rendering legal,
accounting, or other professional advice. If legal advice or other expert assistance is required, the services of
a qualified professional person should be sought.

— From a *Declaration of Principles* jointly adopted by a Committee of the
American Bar Association and a Committee of Publishers and Associations.

This book is available at quantity discounts for bulk purchases. For information, call 1-800-872-5627.

We're grateful to a number of people for helping to make this book a reality. Stacey Miller contributed platefuls of ideas and was a great help in developing the book. Jennifer Stoffel, publisher of *Cleveland Parent*, was also one of our chefs; thanks for helping to cook up ideas and develop the manuscript. And Chris Payack, one of the more creative elementary school teachers on the planet, gave us some terrific food for thought.

Our editor, Brandon Toropov, and publisher, Bob Adams, cheered us on from across the table, while our children, Noah and Audrey, often patiently waited for the table to be set. Thanks, kids!

Introduction

Whatever happened to the family dinner hour, when people sat down together and talked?

It seems that fast food, busy lifestyles, and the necessity of having two income earners have made the family dinner all but a relic of the past. Some people argue that the idea of a sit-down family dinner just doesn't work in today's hustle-bustle world. Others point to the vanishing dinner hour as just another symptom of our deteriorating family structure. And still others apathetically shrug their shoulders and say, "That's just the way things are today, and there's nothing we can do about it."

Regardless of your position on the importance of family meals, it's clear that there *is* something we can do to revive the dinner hour. And that's why we've written this book. We believe that everyone in your household will benefit from a little "table talk"—after-dinner chats and games that give people a chance to spend some time together before retreating to home-work, "work," housework, or whatever people in your family do at the conclusion of a meal.

Table Talk! is designed to provide quick and easy activities—dialogues, role play, games, etc.—that require little or no preparation or props. Occasionally you'll need a newspaper or magazine, pencil or paper, or some readily available household items. But for the most part the idea is to relax and enjoy five or ten minutes just talking and thinking, learning and sharing.

Which brings us to a key point: it's not the quantity of time you spend "table talking," or, for that matter, the frequency—what counts is simply making the commitment however often you can to spend some after-dinner time with your kids and family members without thinking about work, money, errands, or anything else. The idea is simply to "be there" as one of the players, a peer, and a friend. (That's our definition of the often-maligned "Q" term: "quality time.")

Whether your family members' work schedules and social lives permit one night a week for table talk activities or seven nights, whether you can spend five minutes or fifty minutes for each activity session, we think you'll find the experience enjoyable and rewarding. And you might suddenly find yourself having more time on your hands than you expected, time that you can fill with yet additional table talk activities.

In the following pages you'll discover a wide range of activities that fall into twenty-two categories, including:

Cast Your Vote: These activities provide opportunities for your family to vote on issues ranging from favorite books to neighborhood concerns. Just make a ballot box (from a carton or shoebox), provide slips of paper and pens, and let the voting begin.

Dinner Theater: These activities include suggestions for mime, role play, and other forms of entertainment that can be done right at the table—with no props.

 Family Album: In these activities, you'll find "interview" topics ranging from school days to great vacations. Your family "scribe" turns the results into a leaf of a Family Album (a notebook or "blank book").

 Family Book Works: These activities use all kinds of books (storybooks, how-to, reference, etc.) to launch dinner table fun, from learning about new places to performing arts.

 Family Communications: These activities allow you to develop communication skills by composing everything from greeting cards to a family newspaper.

 Family Senate: What "laws" would your family like to enact? Find out with these activities, and get ready for some great orations on your kitchen floor!

 Fifty Questions: The activities in this section consist of a thoughtful question for a family member to pose. Each person then contributes an answer—who knows where the conversation will go!

 Game Time: These activities describe word, memory, storytelling, and various mind games that can be scaled up or down for family members of various ages.

 Gazette Games: As these activities show, a newspaper can be a great avenue not only for learning about the world around us but also for launching hours of fun.

Play School: The family that learns together can have memorable dinnertime fun together. And the best part is that your family will keep coming back for second and third helpings!

Radio Days: Do you have any "hams" in your family? These activities are guaranteed to bring out the journalistic talents and vaudeville skills of everyone at the table.

Shipwrecked: Here's your chance to play Swiss Family Robinson without leaving the table. Each of these activities poses a tantalizing challenge: your family has been whisked away in time or space. How will people use their creativity to cope with their new environment?

Show and Tell: These activities allow your family to share favorite possessions and learn more about each other's interests and likes in the process.

Great Debates: Each activity provides you with a debate topic, along with starter suggestions for "pro" and "con" positions. Your job is to encourage people to support one side or the other, or introduce their own pros and cons.

Great Thoughts: How would you like to bring time-proven words of wisdom to your dinner table? We've assembled some classic proverbs and sayings, followed by thought-provoking related questions for your family to discuss.

Guessing Games: These activities will challenge your family, allow you to call on your reasoning and intuitive skills—and provide great entertainment in the process.

Playalong Junk Mail: Your daily mail delivery can be your special ticket to after-dinner fun. These activities use junk mail for a variety of unusual games. We think you'll find them a neat way to recycle your mail and enjoy the dinner hour at the same time!

Soapbox: If your family members are always in search of a forum for airing their opinions or pontificating about the issues of the day, these activities are for you! Each provides an opportunity for your family to be heard.

Take a Letter: Would your family members enjoy dropping a note to the local paper about something that's happening in your community? Would they like to give a bit of advice? Put down your thoughts with these activities, right at the table.

Time Travel: How would your family like to counter myths and misconceptions of the past with their modern-day education and knowledge? Here's their chance.

Twilight Zone: What would your family members do if they encountered alien life forms or were magically transformed into a school of fish? Find out by exploring these activities.

What's the Plan?: Want to ensure that your family has lots of activities and outings planned for each season? Ask, "What's the Plan?" These activities help you do that by guiding your thinking through all four seasons. Record your ideas in a plan book.

Within each of the activity categories you'll find a variety of subjects, from "Arts and Media" to "Zany Stuff." In between you'll find "Books and Literature," "Careers and Occupations," "History," "Politics," "Readin', Writin', 'Rithmetic," "Science and Nature," "Self and Emotions," and many others (see the Index for a complete breakdown of subjects). Activities that can be easily adapted for younger children are listed under a separate heading in the Index.

We suggest that you thumb through the book and look for the activity categories that will most appeal to your family members. Surprise them with an activity or two, then give a preview of tomorrow's (or next week's) table talk activity. Pretty soon family members may find the dinner hour to be the most special time of the day.

Bon appétit!

Steve Bennett
Ruth Loetterle Bennett

Action Talk!, #1

After-Dinner Speeches, #2

Air Words, #3

Air Your Gripes, #4

Alphabet Animals, #5

Always For Sale, #6

An Apple Every Day, #7

And in the Next Category, #8

An Eye for an Eye, #9

And Diamonds for All, #10

And If I'm Elected . . . , #11

And on That Letter, #12

Animal Awards, #13

Animal Homes, #14

Animal Kingdom, #15

Animal Rights/Wrongs, #16

Anything Goes, #17

Apple Picking, #18

Around the World, #19

Ask Anything, #20

A Station Break, #21

At the
Opera, #22

At the Top, #23

At the Zoo, #24

Attn: Penn
Ave., #25

Autograph
Party, #26

Awards
Dinner, #27

A War to End All
Wars, #28

A Word a Day, #29

B Is for
Beautiful, #30

Back to
Basics, #31

Back to the
Mayflower, #32

Barbecues, #33

Battle of the
Sexes, #34

Be a Part, #35

Be a Sport, #36

Bedtime
Beliefs, #37

Begin at the
End, #38

Being Friends, #39

Best Books, #40

Better with
Time, #41

Beyond
Superstitions, #42

Coupon Concentration, #57

Cultivated Friends, #58

Customer Satisfaction, #59

Cut and Paste Letters, #60

Dear Santa, #61

Dial 911, #62

Dictionary, #63

Changing Places, #50

Choose a Pet, #51

City Smart, #52

Code of Honor, #53

Comic Clips, #54

Community Awards, #55

The Constant Sky, #56

The Big Screen, #43

Capital Mania, #44

Career Night, #45

Catalog Object Watch, #46

Catch up on Books, #47

Categories, #48

Chain Letters, #49

Dirt into
Gold, #64

Discretion
Advised, #65

Dog Days, #66

Do It Well, #67

Double
Standards, #68

Dream Lives, #69

Earn It or Lose
It, #70

The Earth
Moves, #71

Editorials, #72

Empty Tank, #73

Encyclopedia
Roulette, #74

E.T. Come
Home, #75

Exploring the
World, #76

Family
Democracy, #77

Family
Events, #78

Family
Fables, #79

The Family
Herald, #80

Family Tree, #81

Fan Letter, #82

Faux Fur, #83

Film at
Eleven, #84

Getting at the Truth, #99

 Getting to Yes, #100

 Ghost, #101

 Giving and Receiving, #102

 Global Speak, #103

 Going on a Trip, #104

 The Golden Rule, #105

 Friends Indeed, #92

 Future Shock, #93

 FYI, #94

 Garden Cook, #95

 Gender Issues, #96

 Get Out the Vote, #97

 Get Ready for Spring, #98

 Fishing Around, #85

 Food Chain, #86

 Food, Glorious Food, #87

 Forgive and Forget, #88

 For the Birds, #89

 Fortune Cookies, #90

 For What You Believe, #91

The Gold Rush, #106

A Good Heart, #107

Good Listening, #108

Good Morning!, #109

Great American Novel, #110

Great Grammar, #111

Grownups Only, #112

Guess That Recipe, #113

Guess the History, #114

Ham It Up, #115

Hands Up, #116

Hang Onto It?, #117

Headliners, #118

Here's What We've Done, #119

Hidden Treasures, #120

Hidden Words, #121

Holiday Business, #122

Home Alone, #123

Homework Helper, #124

Honesty Is Best, #125

Hooray for Holidays!, #126

How Do You See
It?, #127

How Things
Look, #128

If I Were
President, #129

If It Suits
You, #130

Imagine No
Rules, #131

I'm Thinking
Of . . ., #132

Inch by
Inch, #133

In Good
Time, #134

Initials
Game, #135

In the
Desert, #136

In the Light of
Day, #137

In the
Wilderness, #138

In Which
Room?, #139

I Shall Return . . .
Maybe, #140

Is This the Real
Life?, #141

It Takes
Patience, #142

I Wish . . ., #143

Jot This
Down, #144

Jungle Laws, #145

Junior Moms and
Dads, #146

Junk
Mail, #147

Jurassic Name
Game, #148

Just
Because, #149

Know-It
Alls, #150

Land Before
Time, #151

Land of the
Giants, #152

Language
Lab, #153

"Laws" of the
Land, #154

Leaf
Peeping, #155

Leave 'Em
Laughing, #156

Leisure
Time, #157

Let It Be, #158

Let's Check Our
Book, #159

Let the Good Times
Roll, #160

Library
Weekend, #161

The Life
Of . . ., #162

Life on Mars, #163

Like a
Lion, #164

A Little Bit
Better, #165

Live and
Learn, #166

Living Green, #167

Living Love, #168

Mystery Book, #189

 My Hero, #188

My Favorite Place, #187

My Best Friend, #186

Munching Mandates, #185

Mr. and Ms. Manners, #184

Mousetraps, Etc., #183

Money Isn't Everything, #182

Mixed Emotions, #181

The Midas Touch, #180

Memory Testers, #179

Meet the Aliens, #178

Meeting Friends, #177

Meet a Mime, #176

Making the Grade, #175

Mail Call! #174

Luck of the Draw, #173

Love Is . . ., #172

The Long Way Down, #171

Lonely Hearts Club . . ., #170

Locked Room Mystery, #169

My Turn, #190

Name That Animal, #191

Name That Tune, #192

Nature Care, #193

Neighbor Night, #194

Never Enough Time, #195

Never, Never Land, #196

Newcomers & Old Hands, #197

The New Olympic Games, #198

Next In Line, #199

No-Calorie Menus, #200

No Ifs, Ands, or Buts, #201

Not Always Greener, #202

Note of Appreciation, #203

Nothing to Fear, #204

Not for Prime Time Yet, #205

Now That's Important, #206

Now We're Cooking, #207

Now, What's That Again?, #208

The Old Days, #209

Old Friends, #210

On a Jet
Plane, #211

One Nation, #212

One of a
Kind, #213

On Mount
Olympus, #214

On the
Air, #215

Open
Letter, #216

Oral
Tradition, #217

Our National
Treasures, #218

Ours to
Spend, #219

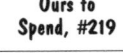

Outer Space, #220

Over the
Rainbow, #221

Parental
Guidance, #222

Parents in the
Midst, #223

Party Time, #224

Pass It
On, #225

Past
Presidents, #226

Past
Vacations, #227

People Polls, #228

People
Prizewinners, #229

Pet People, #230

Pets Talk, #231

Pet
Thoughts, #232

Pioneer
Family, #233

Play Time, #234

Please Say
Thanks, #235

Plot Swap, #236

The Plot
Thickens, #237

Pop Goes the
Quiz, #238

Postcards from
Home, #239

Power
Struggles, #240

Pre-Birthday
Thoughts, #241

Presidential
Honor, #242

Presidents, #243

Protecting a
Friend, #244

A Question of
Cash, #245

Quick to
Forget, #246

Radio Talk, #247

Reaching for the
Stars, #248

Read 'Em and
Vote, #249

Read It or Watch
It?, #250

Read My
Mind, #251

Relatively
Speaking, #252

 **Repeat the Rhythm, #253**

 **Responsible Television?, #254**

 **Right to Vote, #255**

 **Robin Hood, #256**

 **Rocks and Things, #257**

 **Round Robin Alphabet, #258**

 **Rules for the People, #259**

 **Salt, #260**

 **School Days, #261**

 **Schooltime Shopping, #262**

 **Scrambled Story Surprise, #263**

 **See It and Believe It, #264**

 **Seize the Day, #265**

 **Setting the Stage, #266**

 **The Shape Game, #267**

 **Sharing, #268**

 **Sharing Is Caring, #269**

 **Shopping ESP, #270**

 **Shopping for Supper, #271**

 **Silly Recipes, #272**

 **Silly Speak, #273**

Sing for
Me, #274

Siskel and
You, #275

Snowed In, #276

Snow Fun, #277

Song Sense, #278

Sorry!, #279

Space
Explorers, #280

Special
Celebrations, #281

Spelling
Bee, #282

Spending
Spree, #283

Sports
Huddle, #284

Sports
Legends, #285

Sportstacular, #286

State of
Mind, #287

Stay Cool, #288

Straight to the
Top, #289

Strange Transforma-
tions, #290

Stress
Busters, #291

Table Codes, #292

Table Time
Hangman, #293

Tabloid
Journalism, #294

Tabloid
Tales, #295

Take Good
Care, #296

Take It as It
Comes, #297

Talking Through
Clouds, #298

Tall Tales, #299

Tap It Out!, #300

Teach the
Children, #301

Teamwork, #302

Telephone
Chain, #303

That May Live in
Infamy, #304

There Are No Bad
Foods, #305

Things Well
Done, #306

Think
Summer, #307

This Is
A . . ., #308

This Is My
Life, #309

This Just In, #310

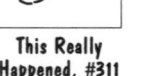

This Really
Happened, #311

Three
Wishes, #312

Three-Letter
Words, #313

Time Capsule, #314

To Add or Not to
Add, #315

To Be
Content, #316

To Tell the
Truth, #317

Tomorrow and
Beyond, #318

Tongue
Twisters, #319

Too Much
Fun, #320

To the
Dump, #321

Transparently
Fun, #322

Travel the
World, #323

Truly Yours, #324

Truth or
Tales, #325

TV Time, #326

Up in
Smoke, #327

Video/Audio
Dinner, #328

Visitor from the
Past, #329

Wagon for
Sale, #330

The Walls Have
Ears, #331

Waste Not, #332

Way-out
Broadcast, #333

The Way
Home?, #334

The Way
We Were, #335

Weather or
Not, #336

Weather Report, #337

Webster's Tales, #338

We the People, #339

What Is Beauty?, #340

What's My Line?, #341

What's That Sound?, #342

What's That You Say?, #343

What's Your Sign?, #344

What Time Is It?, #345

What to Do, #346

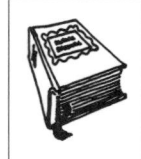

When I Was a Baby I . . ., #347

Where Are You Headed?, #348

Where the Heart Is, #349

Which Way Did It Go?, #350

Who in History?, #351

Who in the World?, #352

The Winner Is . . ., #353

Wish Upon a Star, #354

Women Presidents, #355

Workday Awards, #356

Working on Problems, #357

The World at a
Glance, #358

Worth a
Fortune, #359

Worth a Thousand
Words, #360

The Year
2494, #361

Young and
Old, #362

Your Big
Backyard, #363

You're Cordially
Invited, #364

You're in
Business, #365

Subject: Current Events

Preparation: Scan newspaper, clip articles

Gazette Games

What's the pulse of public opinion in your family about some of the more pressing issues of the day? Find out by having your own "op-ed" session.

Skim the editorial page of your newspaper for subject matter (recycling, energy conservation, teachers' pay, etc.), and bring some of the most interesting topics to the table. (Local papers can be a great source of ideas.) Take turns offering a commentary on the subject. Remember to begin with a headline that summarizes the piece. Then, read the newspaper piece aloud, so people can compare their ideas with those of the pundits. (For younger kids, paraphrase or simply summarize the article.)

Alternatively, you can create your own editorials from scratch. Someone tosses out a headline about a pressing topic not covered in today's newspaper—a pet peeve, a political observation, and so on. Everyone then takes a turn offering commentary. What better way to show your kids the benefits of living in a democracy?

Subject: Zany Stuff

Preparation: None

Dinner Theater

Do you have any budding orators or stand-up comics in your family? Then let them practice public speaking at home, where the critics are kind and there's a never-ending supply of funny material.

Have your family take turns making after-dinner speeches about politics, school, work, everyday activities (such as shopping, getting stuck in traffic, waiting in line, etc.), or anything else that tickles your family's fancy.

Family members can choose their own topics, or for added fun, write down the topics on slips of paper, place the papers in a bowl or bag, and have everyone draw a speech subject.

See how many gifted comedians and speech-makers you have at your house. Then, after they become successful Hollywood performers, you can brag that you knew them when they were just starting out!

3 Air Words

Subject: Readin', Writin', 'Rithmetic
Preparation: None

This dinnertime game puts a new slant on writing with invisible ink. In fact, for this activity, you don't need any ink—all that's required is air!

First, choose someone to start the game off. This person thinks of a word, and "writes" it, letter by letter, in the air—drawing it with his or her finger. The object is for everyone else to take turns guessing what the word is. Of course, if your words are pretty long, you may also want to offer a clue before each round of guessing, such as, "This is a person's name" or, "This is a type of animal." The first person who guesses the word correctly becomes the next "writer."

A variation of this game, especially suitable for new readers, is to start off with letters or numbers, or to limit the word length to, say, three or four letters. For older players, the longer the better. Nothing is more challenging than pulling words out of thin air!

Game Time

Air Your Gripes 4

Subject: Zany Stuff
Preparation: None

We all have our pet peeves—but, when you get right down to it, some of them are quite silly. Here's a dinner table activity that will allow your family members to air their "complaints"—and perhaps even solve every non-problem they can imagine!

Start by having each person "vent" a zany complaint about something in the room where you're sitting. (For instance, perhaps your child wishes that the timepiece on the wall didn't run clockwise.) Then, move on to things in other parts of the house or back yard that "bug" your family.

Have family members take turns posing "solutions" to each problem. (For example, someone might suggest that you turn the clock backwards—then it will run the opposite way!)

So, does your family have any ideas about how to "cure" the houseplants of their tendency to bloom?

Soap Box

Subject: Readin', Writin', Rithmetic
Preparation: None

Here is a guessing game that children of all ages (parents included) will enjoy. All that's required is a working knowledge of the alphabet and the animal kingdom, and your time.

After dinner, have someone think of any kind of animal—pets, farm creatures, birds, fish, etc. Then have other participants guess which animal it is. After each guess, give an alphabet hint. For example, say "porcupine" is the chosen animal. If someone guesses "snake," you say "No, the animal comes before 'snake,'" because "P" comes before "S." If someone guesses "bird," you will tell him or her "No, the animal comes after 'bird,'" because "P" comes after "B."

Tired of animals? You can use other categories as well—foods, cities, names, and so on. Or how about using the titles of some favorite family books, songs, movies, or plays? From *Annie* to *Xanadu*, you're sure to cover a lot of ground before dinner is over!

Category: Just for Fun
Preparation: Clip ads from newspapers and magazines, make a ballot box.

Do you skip over all of the advertisements in newspapers and magazines? If so, then you've been missing a great opportunity for dinner table fun.

Before dinner, ask family members to comb through newspapers and magazines (junk mail is a good resource, too), and clip ads for household gizmos, clothes, cars, etc. Then, after dinner, the family agrees on a set of categories, such as Item Most Worth Saving Up For, Most Unusual Item, Most Useful Item, Most Ingenious Item, Most Useless Item, and so on. Each person then nominates an ad from his or her "hand" for the various categories, after which everyone writes his or her choices on slips of paper and places them in the cardboard voting box.

Then, for added fun, redistribute the ads and create categories from the perspective of some unlikely consumers—the family dog, cat, canary, or pet fish. And if you don't have a pet? Why just reconsider the ads from the point of view of the squirrel or blue jay who lives outside your door!

Subject: Family Circle
Preparation: None

Some experts are recommending year-round school. Would kids learn more and do better without a long summer off? Here are some ideas for starting a table talk debate over the matter.

Leave My Summertime Alone
School is fine, some of the time. Summer is better. Kids need time to express themselves freely, play for hours on end, and be creative and irresponsible. It is during this "free time" that kids learn the most about themselves and life. To take it away would be sad and cruel.

Great Debates

Summer Should Be Shorter
The whole idea of summer vacation sprang from the time when kids were needed at home on the farm to help out with chores during the summer—an outdated concept. Anyway, lots of kids don't really have that much "free time" during the summer but instead are in camp or with caregivers or relatives while their parents continue to go to work. Why not spend more time in school?

Subject: Family Circle
Preparation: Make a ballot box

Here's an election that's sure to bring instant "fame" to all your family members. And everyone is a winner!

Read aloud the name of each family member at your dinner table (and any relatives who aren't present—you can share the results with them later). Then take turns "nominating" categories in which that person might win a prize. For instance, your six-year-old son might be nominated for Best Family Dinosaur Authority, Most Able-Bodied Toybox Cleaner-Upper, and Kindest Older Brother. (Just in case family members are reluctant at first to dish up compliments, have three or four suggestions, on hand for each person—just to show how easy it is!)

Have your family write down each participant's name and their pick for that person's new "title." Sort the votes, and see whether anyone can predict the outcome of the awards before they're announced. Did anyone guess that your three-year-old daughter would get two votes for Best Family Hug-Giver?

Cast Your Vote

Subject: Family Circle

Preparation: None

Great Debates

There's a kid at school who's a real bully—this person pushes, hits, teases, and taunts other kids. Is it okay to fight back? Here are some ideas for starting a table talk debate over the matter.

Bullies Get What They Deserve

If someone is bullying others and is really "asking for it," then someone else is bound to fight back. If the bully is picking on you, then you have no choice but to defend yourself. That's the only way the kid will learn to leave you alone.

Turn the Other Cheek

A bully probably has lots of reasons for acting in a particular way. If someone picks on you, the best thing to do is just to walk away. Sure, you might have to continue to ignore the teasing and taunting for a while, but the other kid will soon tire of the whole thing.

Subject: Self & Emotions

Preparation: None

Great Debates

Diamonds are dazzling, but there are a lot of other pretty things that people can wear as jewelry that aren't as expensive. Which of the following points of view rings true for your family members?

Any Stone Will Do

Why should people want something just because it's so expensive? Why shouldn't people feel proud about whatever jewelry they think looks beautiful on them? When you come down to it, diamonds are no different than any other kind of stone.

Diamonds Are The One and Only

Diamonds are special, partly because they are so expensive and not everyone can afford to buy them. When you have something that costs so much, it sets you apart from everyone else and makes you feel extra good about yourself.

11 And If I'm Elected . . .

Subject: Politics
Preparation: None

Every presidential campaign begins with a platform, including those of your family members running for office.

Have all your family members create platforms for themselves, then take turns giving speeches that explain what they would do if elected to the highest office in the land. Grownups can help younger kids by asking questions for them to answer, such as, Why do you want to be the president? How would you make the world or our country a better place? What would you promise people to get them to vote for you?

Of course, if running for president isn't your goal, you could always campaign for another important office: school principal, mayor, or senator. You can even make up your own position, such as Chief Wake-Up Officer—the person responsible for developing creative and pleasant ways of waking everyone up in the morning!

Soapbox

And on That Letter 12

Subject: Readin', Writin', 'Rithmetic
Preparation: None

These days, there's a newsletter on just about every topic under the sun. Your family can "publish" its own newsletter—and you don't even have to own a computer.

Pick a theme for the newsletter, such as a family vacation, a holiday, or general family news. Then, a designated "editor" can assign stories to family members, or "contributors" can come up with their own story ideas.

Alternatively, you can write story ideas on slips of paper, put them into a bag, and have each family member choose one. Assignments can be kept secret until the writing is done. Then someone can read each story aloud, and everyone can try to guess which family member wrote it.

When the newsletter is written and illustrated, it can be stapled together and later photocopied to be mailed to friends and relatives. "Subscribers" will appreciate being on your mailing list, once they come to find out that your news is good news!

Family Communications

Subject: Science and Nature
Preparation: Make a ballot box

We have contests to choose our favorite songs, movies, plays, and even advertisements. But how often do we take time out to vote for our favorite four-legged creatures and feathered friends? Over dinner, have your family form an Animal Awards Council, and take turns nominating candidates for the following categories (remember, winners can be pets, birds, or even prehistoric creatures—but humans aren't eligible): smartest species, fastest runners, best-looking, most loveable, boldest, most intriguing, master of the skies, and ruler of the farms. (You might want to nominate several in each category to begin with.)

Have council members put their votes into the dinner table ballot box to be tabulated later on. The council can also vote on special neighborhood animal awards, such as most loyal dog, friendliest cat, smartest pet, best-loved animal in your community, most photogenic pet, and most exotic animal. The council can inform the award winners later on—and hope it doesn't go to their heads!

Subject: Science and Nature
Preparation: None

Most of us enjoy visiting a zoo, but what of the animals that live there? Are there any advantages to zoo life? This question can spark some lively dinner table discussions at your house:

Do you think animals in the zoo are happy, or would they rather be back in their natural habitat?

Fifty Questions

15 Animal Kingdom

Subject: Science and Nature
Preparation: Look in a book

Even if your family doesn't have a pet of its own, you can still learn a great deal about animals by reading books on the subject. See what you can find out about your favorite species to share with the rest of your family at the dinner table.

Before you do this activity, assign topics—a favorite mammal, reptile, bird or fish—and have family members take a trip to the library to do some research (or perhaps you can use magazines, books, or encyclopedias from your home library).

You might even want to draw or copy some pictures for "show and tell." Now it's time to share the results. Take turns telling about the animals. Where do

they live? What do they eat? What makes them distinctive? Has anyone in your family ever seen one of these in person? Touched one? Where? When? Would it make a good pet? Why or why not?

Perhaps your family can even plan to visit the zoo and "befriend" the animals themselves!

Show and Tell

Animal Rights/Wrongs 16

Subject: Ethics
Preparation: None

Animals are often used in experiments related to human diseases. Should we use animals for this kind of research? Find out which is your family's pet position.

Animals Have Rights

Animals are living creatures and they ought to have the same rights as humans have. When laboratory animals are injected with diseases to further science, that's unfair. All animal experimentation should be stopped . . . period.

People Have Rights

Using animals to further the cause of science and medicine improves human life. Animal research has ended a lot of human suffering. Are animal rights more important than human rights? Animals are only animals, after all, not people.

Great Debates

Subject: Just for Fun

Preparation: None

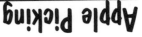

Guessing Games

Sometimes it is the simplest household object that can fascinate our young-sters. This activity may even uncover items you forgot you had!

Choose a person at the dinner table to be "It." This person must then think of an item from around the house—the blender, microwave, the dictionary, or living room sofa. Next, take turns asking questions aimed at identifying the object. Does someone use it daily? Is it new or old? Is it bigger than a breadbox (wouldn't it be interesting if it *were* a breadbox)?

Another way to do this activity, especially with younger kids, is to limit the item chosen to a specific category—say, toys or food items. For older kids, it may be that the more ob-scure the object, the better. How about that old thingamajig in the widget box?

Subject: Science and Nature

Preparation: None

What's the Plan?

Pick-your-own farms have been catch-ing on in recent years. If you haven't yet made fruit picking a seasonal tradition in your family, this plan will get you started.

During this dinnertime conversation, discuss the different things you can make with, say, apples (or any locally grown fruit). Perhaps a day making apple butter will yield this year's Christmas presents for the neighbors. Then select someone as scribe and pull out the plan book. Together, make a list of possible fruit-picking outings. Is there an orchard nearby, or will this mean a day-long trip? Are there any fruit festivals scheduled? With some spe-cific dates in mind, you may want to invite some friends to join you.

Of course, a day of fruit picking means bushels of apples (or some other fruit). Your planning should also include a list of fruit recipes. So, what will be cooking at your house?

Subject: Role Play
Preparation: None

How well could your family communicate, if your survival depended on it?

Let's say that you and your family were riding a plane, and the pilot dropped you off halfway around the world. It's the middle of the night and the dead of winter, and you're dressed for summer. You're cold, hungry, and tired.

There's only one other person around—and he or she doesn't speak your language (any family member can play this

person). How would you and your family tell him or her that you needed warm clothes and jackets? That you needed someplace to spend the night?

That you wanted something to eat—preferably hot soup?

How would you ask your new friend if you could use his or her telephone or car? And if he or she doesn't have (and has never heard of) either—then how would you get him or her to help you make arrangements to go home?

Get set for some highly entertaining role play.

Shipwrecked

Subject: Just for Fun
Preparation: None

Wouldn't it be great to know the answer to the most unanswerable questions? Maybe yes, maybe no. What do your family members think? You'll find out when you ask this dinner table question:

If you could ask the wisest person in the world any one question, what would it be?

Fifty Questions

Subject: Singalong

Preparation: None

Dinner Theater

While some of today's popular bands boast talented vocalists, many of the most highly trained singers perform either at the opera or in stage musicals. If you can't persuade your family to go to the opera or theater, why not bring the music right into your own home instead?

Choose a tale that everyone is familiar with (from a book or the movies, perhaps), an infamous family happening (say, the camping trip where Mom caught a fish that big—but it got away), or a current event (your town's Fourth of July parade or a presidential campaign), and sing about it to the tune of a song you know, or to a made-up melody. You might also create a "chain opera," with your family building a communal melody as each person sings a line or two.

Alternatively, you can set an amount of time—five minutes, perhaps—during which you and your family can communicate only by singing. You might vocalize, "Would someone pass the peas, please?" and your child might warble back, "You said please, so here are the peas. Now, enjoy them, pretty please."

So, Aida and Annie, look out! There's a new family musical production underway that might rival the classics.

Subject: Just for Fun

Preparation: None

Radio Days

If you're tired of hearing ads every time you turn on the radio, here's your chance to clean up the airwaves. Record a worthier commercial—right at your own family radio station.

First, come up with a product that you want to advertise. This can be almost anything that you have handy—food, plates, napkins, or maybe an imaginary invention. Think of some points to make about the product and some interesting ways to deliver your message. Can you write a jingle that will make your product "sell?" What about using sound effects, or demonstrating how the product works? You might also use a tag line in your spot.

There's one thing that you have to watch out for, though. Sometimes, when the commercials get too good, they can be better than the regular programming!

23 At the Top

Subject: Politics
Preparation: None

Naturally, we know what's expected of us—kids go to school, parents raise children and work for a living, and so on. But, what about our nation's leader? Have your family toss around this dinner table question:

What are the most important things the president of our country does?

Fifty Questions

At the Zoo 24

Subject: Science and Nature
Preparation: None

Imagine that you and your family were visiting the local zoo on the last day before it was closed for renovation, and you were accidentally locked in. You look and look, but there's no telephone and no one else is around—it's just you and the animals.

Let's suppose that you and your family decided to turn your plight into a scientific adventure. How could you conduct season-long experiments to answer questions such as: Do animals understand what humans say? Can animals learn to speak a human language? Which animal languages can humans learn to speak? Can animals participate in sports? And who's better at sports—animals or humans?

What other human skills can animals acquire? Can they learn to govern themselves? By the time the season starts again, your local zoo might turn into an Animal Farm!

Shipwrecked

Attn: Pennsylvania Ave.

Subject: Just for Fun

Preparation: None

Have you ever wondered what it would be like to be a kid living in the White House? Perhaps it's time for a friendly letter to the First Family.

To generate ideas for the letter, talk during dinner about what it would be like to live in the White House. Would a First Child have much privacy? Much fun? Many friends? Would he or she miss home? Get into much mischief? Have special privileges? What would your child most want to know about the life of a First Child?

Now, choose a scribe and compose a friendly letter to the First Child. You could ask questions, or maybe even offer some advice. (The address: 1600 Pennsylvania Ave., N.W., Washington, D.C. 20500.)

After signing off, take a family poll: Who thinks you'll get a reply from the White House?

Autograph Party

Subject: Books and Literature

Preparation: Supply paper and pens

Signatures of famous people can be worth a lot to collectors. But even though you'll probably get your family's autographs for free, they can be pretty valuable, too—especially when, years from now, they bring back fond memories.

You can buy "blank books," or better yet make your own by recycling household or office paper. Each person can design his or her own cover by writing "Jane's (or whoever's) Autograph Book," the date, and drawing a picture. Then, get ready to throw an autograph party!

Pass the books around the dinner table, and make sure that everybody gets to sign each one. Have participants write special messages or fun verses and then sign their names below. (Mom or Dad might pull out an old yearbook for inspiration. Remember this one? "I'm the clown who came to town and signed your yearbook upside down.") Then, when the books are all signed, each person can take turns reading the messages aloud. Someday, maybe you'll boast that you held the autograph in your hands when it was just written—and before it became a sought-after collectors' item!

Family Book Works

27 Awards Dinner

Subject: Family Circle
Preparation: Supply paper for family album

If modesty precludes your building a glass-enclosed trophy case to showcase your family's accomplishments, then why not create a subtler version for your family album? (Be sure to leave the first page of the album blank for the "Code of Honor"—see activity #53.)

Describe each family member's awards, including certificates of merit, diplomas, medals, trophies, and so on. What were they for and when were they awarded? Also, have your family acknowledge any formerly unheralded accomplishments ("graduating" to the next reading group, learning to ride a two-wheeled bicycle without training wheels, breaking the family record for "most picture books read," or inventing a new use for recycled yogurt containers).

Leave plenty of room to record each family member's future awards and honors. There's no limit to what your family can achieve!

Family Album

A War to End All Wars 28

Subject: Current Events
Preparation: None

Would wars be necessary if people just sat down and talked about their differences? Here are some ideas for starting a dinner table debate over the matter.

Talk It Out

If we communicated with each other, we wouldn't have to resort to war. Also, if we have a problem (for instance, if there isn't enough water to go around), we'd accomplish more by talking about the problem than by fighting. It would be in everyone's best interest to work things out peacefully.

War Is Inevitable

There are some evil people in this world who only care about staying in power so they can control countries and other people. If such a person is about to do something that will hurt millions of people, shouldn't we try to step in? While people do suffer during (and as a result of) war, wouldn't people suffer more if countries ignored important problems?

Great Debates

Gazette Games

Subject: Just for Fun

Preparation: None

How about learning a new word a day? With the daily newspaper on hand, the words you find are bound to be news-worthy as well.

After dinner, divvy up the newspaper into sections with a few pages passed around to everyone. Then give all dinner table guests a red pencil or crayon so they can circle any words they don't know. Be sure to look at headlines, photo captions, and ads. After everyone has a few new words picked out, take turns around the table trying to figure out what they mean. Does the context offer any clues?

Of course, if the word has everyone stumped, you will need to bring the dictionary to the table. Be forewarned, journalists have been known to coin words and phrases—some might not be in the dictionary!

Fifty Questions

Subject: Self and Emotions

Preparation: None

Some people spend a lot of time groom-ing themselves in the morning so they'll look good. Others say that beauty is in the eye of the beholder. Why not have your family contemplate this question at your dinner table:

What does it really mean to be beautiful?

31 Back to Basics

Subject: School Matters
Preparation: None

There are some people who think that schools spend too much time teaching extra subjects like physical education, music, and art, and not enough time teaching basics like reading, writing, and arithmetic. What does your family think?

Stick to the Basics

If kids don't learn how to read, write, add, and subtract, then they won't be able to work or live normal lives. Schools waste so much time teaching things we don't need that they have no time left over for teaching things that are important.

Great Debates

Get Past the Basics

Physical education, music, art, and other "extras" are important. These are all things that we need in life. We should add even more extras, like how to be a good neighbor—things that would make our lives better. There's more to life than readin', writin', and 'rithmetic.

Back to the Mayflower 32

Subject: History
Preparation: None

What a great opportunity for historical research! Your family has just volunteered to take the first-ever time machine voyage into the past. All dials have been set—for seventeenth-century Plymouth Plantation! There you'll meet the Pilgrims who established the first permanent settlement in the New World during their first Massachusetts winter.

You're scheduled to stay there for one year—although, since no one's ever done this before, there's no absolute guarantee that you'll ever be able to get back.

You can bring with you only as much luggage as you can carry. What kind of clothes will you take? What foods will you take to ensure that you have enough to eat all winter long? What things will you need to make plantation life easier? To build a safe home? To prepare for the seasons ahead? And to take accurate notes on your stay?

Have a safe trip, and we'll look forward to reading your report!

Shipwrecked

33 Barbecues

Subject: Food
Preparation: None

Are your kids picky eaters? Getting everyone involved in the cooking and planning of meals is a sure way to gear up their appetites.

During dinner, discuss the kinds of foods that can be cooked out-of-doors. Perhaps you have an old family recipe for barbecued chicken, or you've always wanted to try grilling corn on the cob or blackened fish. Next, select someone as scribe and pull out your plan book. Together, make up a list of recipes for cooking outside, making sure to include everyone's favorite. Then plan for an outdoor family barbecue, perhaps once a week. Don't forget to assign some duties—like shopping, preparing, cooking, and clean-up. You may even want to invite friends.

This is an activity that can be as simple as cooking burgers and hotdogs every week, or made more elaborate by planning to experiment with new recipes at each barbecue. Perhaps you want to take turns being "chef-in-charge." Just be prepared to eat blackened marshmallows!

34 Battle of the Sexes

Subject: Family Circle
Preparation: None

In these enlightened times, both sexes are treated alike. Right? See whether your family can come to an agreement about this.

No Differences

Men and boys and women and girls are always treated the same in most households. Everyone has the same responsibilities and privileges. Being male or female doesn't make a difference, and it shouldn't.

Great Debates

Big Differences

Males and females are treated differently from each other in many ways. Men and boys are expected to work harder, and they get more independence. Women and girls have lighter chores (they work in the kitchen instead of taking out the trash), but they have less freedom. It's not fair.

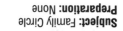

35 Be a Part

Subject: Neighborhood Awareness
Preparation: None

It's easy to get so involved in family life that you forget the community and neighbors around you. This activity will help your family be a part of your neighborhood.

At dinnertime, discuss the neighbors and the community—the problems and issues that concern you. Perhaps someone nearby lives alone or there is an organization that is looking for some help. Then go around the table collecting suggestions for a family policy on involvement. Ideas: help out at an area club or group once a week; take turns helping an elderly neighbor; join an organization as a family and volunteer at special events.

Once you've all settled on an idea, go around the table debating the proposed agenda. Perhaps you've chosen to help clean the local park. Is your goal reasonable? How might your plan be improved? Last but not least, put the plan to a vote—remember, you're all in this together!

Family Senate

Be a Sport 36

Subject: Sports
Preparation: None

Should boys and girls play on the same sports teams—say, on the basketball court or the baseball diamond? Perhaps the issue has already been resolved at some schools—but does your family feel that coed teams are appropriate? Here are some ideas for starting a table talk debate over the matter:

Boys Play Too Rough

The world of sports is very competitive and sometimes very rough—injuries are commonplace. This kind of atmosphere is no place for girls—they would be too easily hurt. And if the sport was "toned down" to accommodate girls' participation, it would be ruined.

Girls Should Get the Same Chance

You cannot decide in advance that all girls are too easily hurt or cannot thrive in a competitive, physical environment. Boys "try out" for teams, so girls should too. And if they cut it, they'll help the team be a winner.

Great Debates

37 | Bedtime Beliefs

Subject: Self and Emotions
Preparation: None

Who, as a child, hasn't wondered about what lurks under the bed, or in the closet? Here's a question your family members can discuss at the dinner table; perhaps it might diffuse a little anxiety:

Some people are afraid of the dark. Why is that?

38 | Begin at the End

Subject: Geography
Preparation: None

Time after time we are reminded that our children aren't learning geography. Well, here's a fun way to extend their knowledge of places—or catch up on the places they know.

After dinner, choose someone to start off the game. That person names a place—any city, state, country, or continent. The next person must then think of a place that begins with the same last letter. For example, the first person might say BostoN. The next person then might say NebraskA. The next person then might say Amster-daM. And so on.

Another way to play this game is to limit the places to a category—such as cities—before you move on to states, countries, and continents.

Before long, you might have some geography wizards right at your table!

Subject: Friendship
Preparation: None

Friendship is an important part of life at every age. Yet most everyone discovers that good friends are both hard to find and hard to keep. This question about friendship is sure to spark a thoughtful dinner table discussion:

What are some things that good friends should do for each other?

Fifty Questions

Subject: Books and Literature
Preparation: Make a ballot box

Why should the folks in Stockholm have the last word on prize-winning literature and authors? You can form a family "Best Books Committee" and honor your own choices for literary greats.

Have committee members nominate favorite books in categories such as: animal stories, mysteries, adventure stories, fairy tales and fables, poetry and rhymes, best author, most likeable leading character, most evil villain, most original plot, most inventive mystery, funniest story, most educational book, greatest bedtime story, neatest pictures, etc. Then, have everyone cast a vote for his or her personal favorite in each category (deposit slips of paper in the dinner table ballot box). After tabulating the votes, have somebody announce the "winners" in each genre. From these, see whether your family can elect one "all-around literary great."

Announce the election results and have someone list all of the "Best Books" winners. And the prize? Why, each will be featured in an upcoming family read-aloud series, naturally!

Cast Your Vote

Better with Time

Subject: Self and Emotions

Preparation: None

W ise words to ponder:

Slow but steady wins the race.

Start a great dinner table discussion by asking:

1. Is it better to go all out and finish a job quickly or do a little bit at a time?

2. Can you think of a time when a chore or project didn't come out as well as it could have because you were in a hurry?

3. What's the best way to slow down when you're in too much of a hurry to get things done?

Beyond Superstitions

Subject: Science and Nature

Preparation: None

Time Travel

I n times past, the rare event of a solar eclipse was viewed as particularly ominous and fearful. Legend after legend reported that an eclipse immediately preceded a disaster or other unusual event.

During this dinner table time travel, imagine that you have been sent to an ancient civilization to explain that solar eclipses are natural phenomena (the moon is positioned in such a way as to temporarily block the sun). To do this, of course, you will probably have to explain something of the positions and movement of the sun, the moon, and the planets.

Once your family has reassured our ancient ancestors about eclipses, you might return to more modern times and try to debunk ideas about walking under ladders, knocking on wood, and tossing salt over your shoulder!

43 The Big Screen

Subject: Arts and Media
Preparation: None

Imagine that you and your family went to see a movie on a Friday afternoon. You stayed until the credits finished rolling, then discovered that you were locked in until Monday! Fortunately, you've got plenty of food to get you through the weekend.

The theater only keeps four movies on hand at any one time (and you just watched one of them). The four films can be whatever you and your family choose, and you can watch them as many times as you like.

Have your family select the four movies. Would you pick films that you'd always wanted to see but never had? Movies that are supposed to be "good for you?" Shows you've seen hundreds of times but never get tired of?

It may be tough to be stranded—but at least you're beating the seven-dollar ticket prices!

Shipwrecked

Subject: Readin', Writin', 'Rithmetic
Preparation: None

How much does your family know about our great states? Here's a way to make a little fun out of learning the state capitals.

After dinner, choose someone (a parent or older child) to act as a moderator. The moderator calls out a state and asks each family member to name the capital, continuing around the table until the correct answer is given. The person who names the most becomes the moderator for the next round.

For reference, here are the capitals of the states:

AL: Montgomery	LA: Baton Rouge	OH: Columbus
AK: Juneau	ME: Augusta	OK: Oklahoma City
AZ: Phoenix	MD: Annapolis	OR: Salem
AR: Little Rock	MA: Boston	PA: Harrisburg
CA: Sacramento	MI: Lansing	RI: Providence
CO: Denver	MN: St. Paul	SC: Columbia
CT: Hartford	MS: Jackson	SD: Pierre
DE: Dover	MO: Jefferson City	TN: Nashville
FL: Tallahassee	MT: Helena	TX: Austin
GA: Atlanta	NE: Lincoln	UT: Salt Lake City
HI: Honolulu	NV: Carson City	VT: Montpelier
ID: Boise	NM: Santa Fe	VA: Richmond
IL: Springfield	NH: Concord	WA: Olympia
IN: Indianapolis	NJ: Trenton	WV: Charleston
IA: Des Moines	NY: Albany	WI: Madison
KS: Topeka	NC: Raleigh	WY: Cheyenne
KY: Frankfort	ND: Bismarck	

Play School

Subject: Careers and Occupations
Preparation: None

What do you do all day? And what will your kids do when they make their way into the world? This activity puts careers under the spotlight.

Adults can begin by talking about their jobs, giving such details as what a day in the workplace is like, what the most important aspects of the job are, what the most challenging responsibilities are, what they like best about the work, what they find the most exciting, and so on. They can also describe their offices or work space and their colleagues, and then field questions from each other and the kids.

As for kids, they can invent careers for themselves, choosing something they might really aspire to become (say, an astronaut, lawyer, or musician) or something zany (a dinosaur feeder, wizard, or dragon catcher). Who knows, you might be surprised to learn that you have a world-renowned doctor or a Pulitzer prize-winning author sitting right next to you.

Finally, you might also take a flight of fancy yourself. Use the activity to describe the career path you might have taken if only . . . .

Subject: Zany Stuff
Preparation: Clip pictures from catalogs

When it comes to high-tech gadgets and oddball innovations, the stranger the object, the more likely it is to be featured in a glossy catalogue that winds up in your mailbox!

Before dinner, distribute your unneeded catalogs to family members and have each person cut out pictures of some modern-day wonder inventions. (Each person is in charge of jotting down or remembering what the objects he or she clipped really do and what they're called.) Then, over dinner, have your family suggest possible names and uses for each picture. For example, you might turn what was a transparent telephone into a combination fishtank/phone. Then you can compare your creations with the real things—the manufacturers' visions can be as fascinating as yours!

You can also have each family member choose an "unidentified catalog object" and "sell" it to the family—the more unlikely the item, the greater the challenge. What could you say to interest your family in a motorized tie rack?

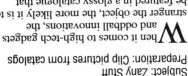

Subject: Books and Literature
Preparation: None

Summer is a great time to read—strictly for entertainment—the books we never seem to find time for during the rest of the year. Have your family make plans to take full literary advantage of the long, lazy days of summer.

At the table, discuss how a book or two could add to the summer's activities or projects. Perhaps there is a subject—astronomy, cooking, gardening—that's not covered in school (yet), or a project—sandbox building, bicycle repair—that will take a bit of research. Is there a novel you've been wanting to "sink your teeth into?" Now select someone as scribe and take out the plan book. Go around the table creating a summer reading list. Perhaps you'll also want to plan a weekly family trip to the library.

With a reading plan in hand, you'll be set for a summer's worth of great literary adventure!

What's the Plan?

Subject: Just for Fun
Preparation: None

This activity can be as simple or as complicated as your family decides. However you play, you are sure to learn something about your best subjects.

Choose someone to pick a category, like "vegetables," "countries," or "dinosaurs." Then, go around the table and take turns giving examples of things in that category; for example, carrots, turnips and squash, or France, Germany, and Spain. The round continues until someone is stuck without an example—the object is to not be that person!

Take turns deciding on a category. For older children, choose categories that will stimulate their imaginations and challenge their minds. How about "exotic undersea life forms?"

Game Time

49 Chain Letters

Subject: Readin', Writin', Rithmetic
Preparation: None

Game Time

This activity requires only hands and backs. That means that you can do it at a moment's notice—just as long as your hands are free!

During this dinnertime game, go around the table taking turns "writing" or "tracing" a letter on the next person's back. Keeping silent, that person then guesses what the letter is and in turn "writes" the same letter on the next person. Finally, the last person at the table guesses out loud what the letter was. How close is it to the original?

Another way to do this game—and to involve early readers and writers—is to "write" the letters on the back of each person's hand instead. That way you can not only feel the shape but also see the letter being "written." (Older kids might want to add more mystery by writing on the guesser's hand under the table.)

Now, tonight's menu doesn't include finger foods, does it?

50 Changing Places

Subject: Family Circle
Preparation: None

What would happen if everyone in your family traded places? Now's your chance to find out!

Have everybody write his or her name on a slip of paper, fold the slip in half, and put it into a paper bag. Each person chooses a name and then becomes that family member. (If you choose your own name, return it and pick another.) Act out a familiar situation—say, getting ready to go to school or work, driving home from a movie, or eating a meal at home or in a restaurant. What would he or she do and say in that situation? For even more of a challenge, choose names but don't tell each other which person's you drew. See whether family members can guess, just by watching and listening, who you are portraying.

You might find that trading places is a great treat, or you might come to appreciate who you are even more.

Dinner Theater

51 Choose a Pet

Subject: Just for Fun
Preparation: None

We know that many people have pets like cats, dogs, goldfish, and parakeets. But what makes an animal a pet? Ask your family this question at the dinner table:

Why do people keep some animals as pets but let others remain in the wild?

Fifty Questions

City Smart 52

Subject: Geography
Preparation: Look in a book

How would you like to see the rest of the country—right from your dinner table? Here's an activity that gives your children the opportunity to learn about different places and to share the information with the rest of the family.

"Assign" states (or find out which states family members are most interested in learning about) a day or so before. Then, at the dinner table, share the information you've gathered: the state's capital, its major industries, its geography, climate, and so on. Pass around any pictures you photocopied or drew—that will help family members to visualize what the state is like.

If anyone in the family has actually been to the state, have that person discuss what it's like from an "insider's" perspective. What was his or her impression? Would he or she want to visit there again? Perhaps he or she would even like to live there some day—and you can come for a surprise visit.

Show and Tell

53 Code of Honor

Subject: Family Circle
Preparation: None

Has the idea of living true to a code of honor gone out of style? How about your family—do you have a shared outlook? A set of ideals?

During and after dinner, poll the family for a shared credo of sorts to include as a list of "Ten Things We Stand For" in your new Family Album. Go around the table and take turns thinking of attitudes that you value in your family. Then, pick a scribe (an older child or parent) to write down your list. Does the order matter? Do you only have one or two codes to live by?

As this is to become page number one of your Family Album, allow younger children to get in the act by adding an illustration.

Another way to enjoy this activity is to tell (and write down) a story about each of your family's shared ideals. Perhaps you can remember a time when Good Humor got everyone through a difficult time!

54 Comic Clips

Subject: Story Making
Preparation: Collect and clip comic strips

Does your family faithfully follow the adventures of dancing beagles and talking cats? Some cartoonists have invented new plots for their characters each day for years, and they never run out of ideas. Can your family help out by coming up with your own story, just once?

Have someone read aloud the first frame of your favorite comic strip and describe the picture. Players then make up the rest of the story. Each person takes a turn at describing the action and supplying a caption until the story is complete. Compare your story with the plot of the original strip. Which do you like better?

Alternatively, each family member can draw a picture and write the caption. These can either be shared on the spot or put into a bag, mixed up, and read in any order to make a story that's funny, serious, or just plain silly.

Be warned though: after this, you and your family may never look at the Peanuts gang in the same way again!

55 Community Awards

Subject: Neighborhood Awareness
Preparation: Make a ballot box

What are the best but oft-ignored aspects of your neighborhood? Have your family take time to honor some of them at the dinner table.

Ask family members to nominate community highlights: Tallest Building, Most Beautiful Landscaping, Best Shop, Wildest Paint Job, Coolest Car, Best Animal Hangout, Most Improved House, Most Interesting Walking Route, and Best View in Town. (If your family is stuck for ideas, see whether you can offer three or four suggestions for each category yourself.) Cast your votes in a secret ballot, tally them up, and declare the winners.

You can then make certificates to post in honor of the community award winners. Can you imagine hanging a sign on your window that says, "In recognition of the best view in the neighborhood?"

Cast Your Vote

The Constant Sky 56

Subject: Self and Emotions
Preparation: None

Wise words to ponder:

The sky is the same color wherever you go.

Start a great dinner table discussion by asking:

1. Do people believe that changing their situation (changing houses, schools, jobs) will solve all their problems? Why?

2. What are a few things that can change when someone moves . . . and some things that will probably stay the same?

3. How would the world be a different place if everyone accepted what they couldn't change?

Great Thoughts

Subject: Just for Fun

Preparation: Collect and/or clip coupons

If you're overwhelmed by more coupons than you know what to do with, then here's an idea: try committing all of them to memory—well, sort of!

Arrange five coupons on the dinner table so that everyone can see and study them. Then, after the meal, have someone remove one of them while the rest of the family closes their eyes. Now have everyone open his or her eyes. Who can tell which coupon is missing? Was that too easy? Then try using six coupons, then seven, and so on, until you see how many it takes to stump your whole family.

Now see whether your family can concentrate on saving money!

Subject: Family Circle

Preparation: None

Wise words to ponder:

Friendship is a plant we must often water.

Start a great dinner table discussion by asking:

Great Thoughts

1. What kinds of attention do you expect from your friends?

2. If you forget your friends (or vice versa) what happens to the relationship?

3. How about the family—does it require the same attention as your friends to grow and stay healthy?

Subject: Family Circle
Preparation: None

Is there a certain brand of cereal or snack that is an all-time family favorite? If so, why not write a letter of satisfaction? Who knows, you may even get a nice response!

Over dinner, poll the family for favorite brands—maybe it's a kitchen staple, like a certain kind of peanut butter, or a cereal that is always on hand.

Select one item, then choose a scribe (an older child or parent) to write a letter to the company saying how much the product is appreciated and enjoyed. To get everyone in the activity, make sure to give each family member a chance to contribute his or her reasons that the product made the top pick list.

Of course, this activity doesn't have to be about food at all. Anything that continues to help the family or make household tasks a little easier could be cause for such a letter. What about smooth-working ballpoint pens and other writing instruments?

Take a Letter

Subject: Readin', Writin', 'Rithmetic
Preparation: Collect junk mail

If you've fallen into the habit of tossing out your junk mail unopened, then you've been missing a lot of fun!

Before dinner, have your older kids open some junk mail and cut the solicitation letters into sections—letterhead, logos, salutations, paragraphs, and so on. Then, at the dinner table, see whether your family can make a wild composite letter by mixing and matching the "spare parts."

Your family can also combine other junk mail components—envelopes, brochures, business cards, post cards, letters, and so on—to make their own zany solicitations.

Have your family members practice putting together zany packages, and who knows? One of them might someday land in the advertising world and put those skills to use every day!

Playalong Junk Mail

Subject: Just for Fun

Preparation: None

A re you barraged at Christmastime with questions about the details of Santa's life up in the North Pole? Here's a way to tackle the questions as well as have some fun.

Go around the table and think of all the questions you have about Santa, Mrs. Claus, the reindeer, and life in general at the North Pole. Choose an older child or parent to be the scribe and write down the questions in a letter format. Younger children might enjoy decorating the letter with crayons or stickers and making it a kind of pre-Christmas greeting.

Of course, you can do this activity any time, not just December. Compose a friendly letter to Santa, checking up on his health and well-being during the off-season. Just what does the Claus family do during August?

Subject: Family Circle

Preparation: None

D o your kids know all the important phone numbers they should? This activity will help you find out—and it's especially well-suited to younger family members.

First, decide on the important numbers. These might include:

■ 911
■ 0 for operator
■ parents' work phone
■ a neighbor
■ a grandparent or other local relative
■ a close friend of the family

Family Communications

Work together to help all family members learn each one. Try creating mnemonics, songs, poems, or whatever is age-appropriate. Then have a "scribe" create a phone list that can be posted near each phone in the house—younger kids can help decorate the list with pictures that help them remember what each phone number means.

By the way, for the youngest kids, don't forget one key addition to the list—your own phone number!

63 Dictionary

Subject: Books and Literature
Preparation: Minimal

Have you ever searched your vocabulary for the perfect word to describe something, like "eudaemonia" (happiness), "trenchancy" (intelligence), and "filiation" (children)? Then this is the game for you.

Have the keeper of your family dictionary (you can take turns) find an unfamiliar word and say it aloud. If anyone at the table knows it already, the keeper must try another word. When a word has been selected, the keeper writes the definition on a sheet of paper, then folds the paper in half and puts it in a paper bag or envelope while everyone else is writing down what he or she thinks the word means (or what the word should mean). All the players then fold their papers and place them in the bag with the original sheet containing the definition. Finally, the dictionary keeper retrieves the papers and reads them all aloud.

Did anybody write down the correct definition? Did anybody find a "better" definition for the word? (For instance, even though "pulchritude" really means beauty, we decided at our house that it ought to be used to describe sharp cheese!)

Family Book Works

Dirt into Gold 64

Subject: Zany Stuff
Preparation: None

How well do you know the inner imaginings of the members of your family? Just what do each of you ponder? You'll know more after your family replies to this question at the dinner table:

What are three impossible things—three things that just couldn't happen?

Fifty Questions

Subject: Arts and Media
Preparation: None

Great Debates

These days, there's a lot of commotion about whether or not television networks should display ratings or warnings before shows air. Some experts say that these steps are necessary to protect children from watching violence on the tube. Others say it's a waste of time to air ratings and warnings. What does your family think?

Ratings and Warnings Are a Good Idea

Children shouldn't be exposed to violence on television. There's so much violence in the real world—who needs more? It's the responsibility of networks to warn parents about violent shows.

Why Bother?

Kids are going to watch what they want to anyway—with or without ratings and warnings. Parents can't be around all the time to control the television set. Besides, what the networks are proposing is unfair—news shows, which wouldn't have to be singled out for violence, are just as violent as some television shows.

Subject: Money Matters
Preparation: None

What's the Plan?

What to do on one of those lazy summer days? Why not plan a garage sale. It will not only be great fun for your kids, but you might get your basement cleaned out at the same time.

Conduct a dinner-time planning session during which your family decides such questions as: Will you go "solo," or ask other families to join in the sale? What day and time will you sponsor the event? Where will you hold it—the backyard, front yard, driveway, etc.? Who will make the signs and where and when will you put them up and take them down? Who will write the tags for the items? What will you use for a cash box? Will you have a "freebie table?" What will you do with items you can't sell—take it to a shelter, church, or some other organization? What will you do with the proceeds—spend it on something the family has been wanting, put it into a fund for a future vacation, etc.?

Finally, get down to the big question: who will tend the lemonade stand?!

67 Do It Well

Subject: Family Circle
Preparation: None

Wise words to ponder:

If a job's worth doing, it's worth doing well.

Start a great dinner table discussion by asking:

1. Have you ever met someone who didn't seem to like their work? What are the hard parts that might make them feel that way? What are the enjoyable parts that might make them want to do the best possible job?

2. Can you think of something good about the chores you like the least—could that help you do them better?

3. What if everyone did just sloppy work—the dishes only partially washed, the laundry all mixed together and the garbage taken out only when it overflowed? Can you describe how different things would be if people didn't try to do their best?

Great Thoughts

Double Standards 68

Subject: Ethics
Preparation: None

Do grownups and children live by the same rules? If not, should they? This question can be instructive for adults and kids alike:

Do all grownups tell the truth all the time—and how do you know?

Fifty Questions

Subject: Just for Fun

Preparation: None

Fifty Questions

What are dreams, where do they come from, and what can we learn from them?

We all dream every night, even we can't always remember what we dreamed. Perhaps your family members have some insights into this mysterious phenomenon of the human mind. Find out by asking this question:

Subject: Family Circle

Preparation: None

Is a regular allowance something that just comes from being part of the family or is it money earned for jobs performed? Here are some ideas for starting a table talk debate over the matter:

An Allowance is Deserved

Kids should automatically receive some kind of allowance—that's just fair. Otherwise they'll have to depend on their parents whenever they want to buy a treat or snack.

Great Debates

An Allowance is Earned

Receiving an allowance should be a direct result of doing work around the house. Being part of the family means being responsible for helping around the house; parents should figure out a fair amount of allowance based on the kids' contributions.

Subject: Science and Nature
Preparation: None

For millenia, people believed that the earth was at the center of the universe. Made sense, of course.

During this dinner table time travel, imagine you have been sent back to the year 1500 to help the mathematician Nicolaus Copernicus explain to the world that the earth orbits the sun and not the other way around. This notion was so dangerous in Copernicus's day that he was forced to delay publication of his "insane claim" about a "heliocentric" universe. And when he did finally publish his ideas, he got into deep trouble with the authorities. How would your junior scientists support Copernicus's theory?

Time Travel

Subject: Current Events
Preparation: None

One way to show your kids that their opinions matter is to help them express themselves. A letter to the editor is the perfect chance to be heard.

After dinner, bring the newspaper to the table and have someone read through the headlines. Pick an appropriate article or two to read aloud and discuss. If there are two sides to the story, there are bound to be some differences of opinions. Choose a spokesperson and help him or her pen a letter to the local newspaper editor voicing your collective concerns. Use the letter-writing time as an opportunity for everyone to help fine-tune the missive. Read it aloud at the table.

Of course, your family may not need to use the newspaper to get started on this activity. A letter to the editor can be about anything. But try to stick to something that you feel strongly about. Then let your thoughts be heard by all!

Take a Letter

Subject: Just for Fun

Preparation: None

Imagine this: you and your family go for a Sunday drive and take a wrong turn onto a deserted road. You drive for some time, then lo and behold, you run out of gas. Unfortunately, you don't have a cellular telephone. But you and your family do have one ace up your sleeves: the ability to conjure up anything that you want just by wishing for it. What would you gin up (other than a tank of gas or a communication device) that could help you out of your plight? Is there anything that could help you attract the attention of potential rescuers? What would you create to help you pass the time until help arrived?

Subject: Just for Fun

Preparation: None

Family Book Works

The encyclopedia is one bookshelf resource that often doesn't get used to its full potential. Here's a fun way to explore this wonderful font of knowledge.

After dinner, excuse everyone from the table for a moment to bring back a volume of the encyclopedia (any reference book will do, really). Then, back at the table, take turns flipping to any page to find a new subject to explore. See whether anyone can answer questions about the subject. Say, "Where is the Parana River?" (South America) or "Why should we remember Paul Dirac?" (He formulated a theory of quantum mechanics.) "What was the Edict of Nantes?" (A decree that established the right of French Protestants to worship freely.)

Another way to do this activity is to choose one person (an older child or adult) to be keeper of the reference books and have everyone else think randomly of subjects they'd really like to understand better. Even the youngest players will find this an exciting way to learn something new.

Subject: Science and Nature
Preparation: None

Some people believe in UFOs and life on other planets. Others think that human beings are alone in the universe. Your family can have an out-of-this-world discussion about this exciting topic.

We're All Alone
There are no such things as extraterrestrials, except in movies and books and on television. If there are aliens, then why hasn't anybody ever been able to meet them? Space creatures and extraterrestrial craft are just figments of our imagination.

Great Debates

The Final Frontier
Although we haven't yet proved that there's life on other planets, we shouldn't rule out the possibility. Besides, many UFO sightings are still unexplained. We've really just begun to explore space. Who knows what we'll find in the years ahead outside our solar system? Anyway, with all the celestial bodies in the universe, some of them must have living beings.

Subject: Geography
Preparation: None

Among western cultures, the idea that there were other people in the world, developing separately with different ideas and beliefs, was rejected for thousands of years. When explorers took off on their expeditions, they were not expecting to find people!

During this dinner table time travel, imagine that you have been sent to Italy in 1272 to help Marco Polo, upon his return from China, convince the folks at home that he did indeed visit the extravagant court of the Chinese emperor Kublai Khan in Peking (now Beijing). How could he have traveled so far? How could another culture—and one that sounds so far-fetched—exist? Perhaps you could describe cultures whose customs are very different from our own in terms of dress, food, and language. Your kids may have some great tidbits of information to pass on to Mr. Polo's sponsors!

Time Travel

Subject: Family Circle
Preparation: None

If your family is like most, you've no doubt been in a situation in which people want to do different things at the same time. Which is more fair, going with the majority rule, or waiting for a unanimous decision? Here are some starter points for this lofty debate.

Great Debates

The Majority Rules

It's easier to get a majority rule than unanimous agreement, so you don't waste time. Even though some people might not get what they want this time, you can always take turns and do what the others want next time.

All or Nothing

This takes time and patience, and means that everyone has to listen to everyone else's views. But in the end, everyone gets what he or she wants. While the majority rule can lead to disappointment, the unanimous rule means that everyone will come out happy with the decision.

Subject: Family Circle
Preparation: None

Family Album

Here's a way to capture some of your family's best times together and preserve them in your Family Album.

Over dinner, have family members list occasions that roll around every year, and describe how they're celebrated in your family. For instance, do you stay at home, watch the Orange Bowl, and eat Mom's turkey on Thanksgiving along with a couple dozen cousins, aunts, uncles, and grandparents, or do you spend the day skiing on the slopes of Vermont? Include any other special traditions: Is there any family besides ours that saves the seeds from jack-o-lanterns, mixes them with peanut butter, then uses the mixture to stock the backyard bird feeder?

You can also create a "diary" of family holidays, birthdays, anniversaries, and occasions from the past year (or as far back as you can). Include as many details as you can remember, such as dates, guest lists, how everyone dressed, what they ate, the weather, and so on. No event is too small to note. Leave room so that, as new events occur, you can record them in your Family Album, too. Who would want to miss the chance to capture the next Children's Day celebration at your house?

Subject: Books and Literature
Preparation: None

Every culture has its own mythology—and now your family can have its own, too.

Begin by telling your version of a popular myth or fable. You can add new characters and endings to give the story a unique twist. For instance, wouldn't it be interesting to hear how Dad craved a bunch of grapes that were just out of his reach, and then decided that the grapes were probably sour anyway? How about the time Mom pulled a nail from a lion's paw and the lion was so grateful that it not only decided to spare her, but gave her a ride to work when the car wouldn't start?

Whether the theme is "turn the other cheek," "slow but steady wins the race," or "two wrongs don't make a right," the family fable is an opportunity to teach your children important values while creating enduring family legends.

Soapbox

Subject: Current Events
Preparation: None

Are you tired of reading the same depressing news day after day? Then create a family newspaper.

Each family member is designated "editor" of his or her own section. Older kids can write their sections, younger children can either dictate their news for someone else to write down or provide hand-drawn "photos."

Here are some ideas to get you started: Education—what's going on in school; Workplace—what Mom and Dad are doing at work; Entertainment—fun things family members have done recently or are planning to do; Food—new favorite recipes and recent family eating trends; Travel—a summary of trips the family has taken recently or is planning to take; Home—home improvement projects that have recently been completed or are underway; Front Page—all the breaking family news.

Staple the completed sections together and you now have the best news in town!

Family Communications

Fan Letter

Subject: Just for Fun

Preparation: None

Take a Letter

Some people say we don't have enough heroes these days. Maybe so, but there are bound to be some celebrities who have captured the admiration of your family. Here's a chance to let them know; maybe you'll even get a response!

During dinner, take turns picking a celebrity the whole family can admire—an actor or a sports figure, an artist, author—whatever. (If you can't agree, you can always pick more than one.) Choose a scribe and dictate a letter telling your hero why you admire him or her. Is the person helping make the world a better place? Is he or she just cheering things up a bit? Or is he or she a role model—someone who is doing what you would like to be able to do?

Whoever you choose, there are bound to be some surprises!

Family Tree

Subject: Family Circle

Preparation: None

Do your kids know your family is a part of history—family history? After dinner, choose someone (a parent or older child) to conduct a research lesson about your family tree. The "teacher" then queries everyone at the table about his or her knowledge of the family and its history. Begin with the people at the table, listing their birth dates and places; then literally branch out from there, listing cousins, aunts, uncles, grandparents—maybe even great-great-grandparents. With some knowledge of when and where they lived, you can perhaps come up with some ideas about what their lives were like.

You might also want to draw the tree on a piece of poster-board, leaving places for photographs and a brief story about each person—what a delightful surprise it will be for visiting relatives!

Subject: Current Events
Preparation: None

Is it okay to wear fur coats and jackets? Is faux fur a better way to go? Here are some ideas for starting a table talk debate over the matter:

Fur Coats Are OK

We use animal products for all sorts of things—shoes, luggage, belts—there is no real difference in using animal fur for coats. Often the animals are raised specifically for their fur. When we refuse to buy fur products, we take jobs away from people who need them.

Leave the Animals Alone

Animal-fur coats are often the result of illegal poaching of endangered species. But even if the animal isn't endangered, it's wrong to kill it for any reason, especially for making luxury clothing. People ought to wear fake fur, or no fur at all.

Great Debates

Subject: Current Events
Preparation: None

Who says that no news is good news? You're in charge of the facts when you "tape" your own newscast.

First, pull together your news team over dinner. You'll want co-anchors who can give the community and world news, and reporters who can handle the weather, traffic, and sports. It also helps to have a director who can "check" the sound levels, let everyone know when the show is about to start, and tell each reporter when it's his or her turn in the hot seat.

Then "produce" a dinner table newscast. Your news can be the real thing, if you've been following current events (you can scan a newspaper before your broadcast to get some ideas), or it can be the product of wishful thinking or your imagination.

At our station we once reported that the wooly mammoths were about to face off against the cave bears, but the game was called due to a fast-moving glacier. That's the way it was . . . and now, back to you.

Dinner Theater

Subject: Just for Fun
Preparation: None

Abracadabra! You and your family have been turned into a school of fish! Have your family discuss the following:

What would a typical day in your lives be like if you lived underwater? What would be the advantages? The disadvantages? What sorts of things that you can do as humans would be impossible as fish? And vice versa? What would be the silliest thing you can imagine happening? And here's a tough one: how do you think you would feel about humans?

Finally, do you think that young fish should have to go to school? After all, they have to live in one!

Subject: Science and Nature
Preparation: None

More and more our youngsters are being taught about the ecological balance of nature. Perhaps a little drama will add to their understanding.

During dinner, family members can cast themselves as links in the food chain. For example, the first person might decide to be an earthworm. He or she might say, "I get all the nutrients that I need from the soil." The next person might choose to be a bird, and say, "I snack on earthworms, but I'm open to eating seeds and various bugs as well." You can follow the food chain all the way up to the largest critter, seeing how many links you can find. To spark an interesting discussion, have one family member temporarily leave the table. What effect would that have on the food chain?

Finally, you might want to take out crayons and drawing paper and have family members create some pictures of the food chain in progress. How would your family do artistic justice to Dad, the spider?

87 Food, Glorious Food

Subject: Food
Preparation: Provide paper for family album

For many people, the aroma of a freshly baked cake brings to mind happy memories—birthday parties, after-school snacks, Grandma's house, and so on. What other foods have personal associations for your family?

Devote a page in your Family Album to food memories. Have each person at the dinner table choose a food (or two), and tell the scribe and the rest of the family the special meaning the food has for him or her. Perhaps the aroma of pancakes frying brings to mind lazy Sunday brunches, the scent of coffee reminds you of heart-to-heart chats with friends, and scoops of ice cream evoke memories of carefree summer days.

You might want to prompt younger children by asking questions such as, "What holiday were we celebrating the last time we had turkey?" or "What foods did we take with us to the Fourth of July picnic?"

This might also be a great place to preserve classic family recipes—homemade ice cream, peanut butter and banana sandwiches, holiday cookies, etc. After all, a family is what it eats!

Family Album

Forgive and Forget 88

Subject: Family Circle
Preparation: None

Wise words to ponder:

He that forgives gains the victory.

Start a great dinner table discussion by asking:

1. Have you ever held a grudge against someone for something the person did a long time ago? How did it make you feel?

2. When you're the first to make up with a friend, how do you feel?

3. If forgiving is such a good feeling; why is it so hard to do?

4. How would the world be different if people forgave each other more easily?

Great Thoughts

Fortune Cookies

Subject: Family Circle

Preparation: None

Game Time

Here's how you can determine your family's fortunes right at the dinner table! Pass around paper and envelopes to everyone at the dinner table. Then have each person write down his or her forecast for the future. In the tradition of "cookie messages," these fortunes should be generic enough to apply to everyone—for instance: "Smile, and you will make the whole world smile with you," or "You can expect great things from people you do not yet know," or "You will soon meet a bear." Next, fold and put the messages in envelopes, and have each person pick a "fortune cookie" to read aloud.

Another way to do this activity is to make some personalized forecasts. Have everyone in the family choose a participant and write down his or her "fortune" (say, "You will soon find something you thought you had lost."). Place all the fortunes in sealed envelopes and designate each with the correct name. Then, in a couple of weeks, open the envelopes and read the fortunes aloud. Did any of the predictions come true? Perhaps your family has a future in the fortune-telling business!

For the Birds

Subject: Science and Nature

Preparation: None

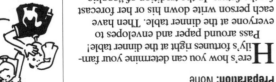

What's the Plan

Imagine weathering the outdoors through the long cold winter. How do the birds manage? With some planning on your part, you can help.

During this dinner table conversation, consider the difficulty the winter weather creates for all the creatures living out of doors. Then invite each family member to come up with an idea for making sure the birds have enough food to eat until spring. After selecting someone as scribe, take out the plan book and make a list of possibilities. Do you need to make a bird-feeder? Perhaps family members can take turns being in charge of restocking the feeder for a week. Impress upon your children the importance of making a serious commitment to the feeding effort; once you start, the birds will become dependent on you. If you don't have a backyard haven, there are other opportunities. Come up with a plan to visit a nearby wild animal shelter, wildlife preserve, or even a city park—equipped with a bag of goodies, of course!

91 For What You Believe

Subject: History
Preparation: None

Everyone disagrees now and again, and sometimes arguments escalate into fights of one kind or another. Are clashes between people inevitable? How about between countries? Try posing this dinner table question to your family:

Why do countries fight wars?

Fifty Questions

Friends Indeed 92

Subject: Family Circle
Preparation: None

Wise words to ponder:

A friend in need is a friend indeed.

Start a great dinner table discussion by asking:

1. Why do people need friends?

2. Is it hard to ask someone for help? Is it easier to ask a friend?

3. Can you list two or three things you have done for a friend lately?

4. What are several things you could do for one of your good friends to show them you care about them?

Great Thoughts

Subject: Zany Stuff
Preparation: None

If we're still broadcasting radio shows in the year 3492, what shows can we look forward to hearing? Experiment with your own talk and tunes of the future.

Your family radio station can transmit news, editorials, weather, traffic reports, and commercials—all from the future. Perhaps the world has united into one global nation and the news of the day focuses on the latest tribunal meeting of the twelve co-leaders. Perhaps cars have become airborne and traffic reports warn of heavily "birded" altitudes to avoid. Commercials might describe great sales on common household appliances—long-range transporter shoes, compact time machines, and solar-powered personal rejuvenation devices (PRDs). In the sports department, your older kids might enjoy reporting on the time-travel basketball playoffs.

And what about the music of the day? Have your family jam on a tune or two. Now, clanging two spoons together won't offer nearly the exhilarating beat of a fusion-powered seventy-three-stringed guitar. But it will provide fine accompaniment for that romantic old song about the polar caps of Mars.

Subject: Current Events
Preparation: None

When radio stations are licensed, they agree to devote some of their time to airing public service announcements. To satisfy these requirements, your family radio station can plan to air its own PSAs.

The spot can be about anything that matters to you and your listening audience. Often it's a helpful tip that you pass along. PSAs might advise people to reuse and recycle or fasten seat belts; they can focus on almost anything that's important to your family.

You might enlist a "celebrity" to speak about an important cause. For instance, have a family member play a prominent politician, telling the audience to "get out and vote in the next election." Or have a sports star talk about the importance of supporting physical education in schools. The possibilities are endless.

Radio stations often air PSAs at odd hours—say, in the early hours of the morning—but you can air yours at any time. All you need is a cause that you believe in, and you're off and running!

95 Garden Cook

Subject: Food
Preparation: None

Harvesting a garden can be one of the highlights of the summer. And you can boost the excitement with a little harvest planning.

During this dinnertime conversation, discuss how the garden crops are progressing. Will there be a bumper crop of tomatoes? Berries? Then select someone as scribe and pull out your plan book. Go around the table and create a list of cooking/preserving projects using the garden's bounty. Tomato sauce, jams or butters, and zucchini bread are all possibilities. (If the discussion catches on, you may want to bring a cookbook to the table for new ideas.) Make sure you assign duties—harvesting, cleaning and cooking—and get everyone involved.

If you don't have a crop or two from your own garden, you can still enjoy the fruits of summer by planning a day or two when you visit a pick-your-own farm or orchard. The biggest challenge will be resisting the temptation to devour all the fruit on the ride home!

What's the Plan?

Gender Issues 96

Subject: Self and Emotions
Preparation: None

Does your family ever feel as though "the other guys" have it easier, and that the grass is greener on the other side of the fence? If so, here's a dinner table question that's sure to spark a lively debate at your house:

Who has more fun—girls or boys—and why?

Fifty Questions

Subject: Current Events
Preparation: None

Elections are a perfect opportunity to learn more about what's important to your family.

Open up this dinnertime conversation with a discussion of some of the national or community issues that have been on your minds. Perhaps it's recycling, the rising number of homeless, or even the cost of health care. This may be a good time to bring a newspaper to the table—headlines can be good conversation starters. Then choose someone as scribe and pull out the plan book. Make a list of ways your family can get involved in the upcoming elections. How will you keep informed? Is there a particular candidate or issue you would like to support? Perhaps you would like to volunteer to help on a local campaign.

Whatever you decide to do, this activity will provide a good beginning in learning something of how our political system works, and how we can all participate in the democratic process.

Subject: Science and Nature
Preparation: None

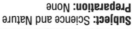

What's the Plan?

Part of the fun of winter is thinking ahead to spring. With a garden plan in hand, you'll have even more to look forward to.

Open up this dinnertime conversation with a discussion of your garden space and what you would like to grow this spring. Choose someone as scribe and take out the plan book to make a list of activities to get your garden started. (You may want to bring a plant and seed catalog or two to the table for ideas.) Select the kinds of plants—vegetables, flowers, herbs—that you want to include and decide which could be started inside from seeds. Have everyone make a commitment to spending some time planting and caring for starters.

If you don't have a lot of space, try planning for a container garden. Plenty of plants can thrive in small tubs or large pots—herbs can even do well on a window sill.

Now, who's going to be in charge of sampling the harvest in the summer?

Subject: Just for Fun
Preparation: None

We seem to know a lot about the age of dinosaurs, except for the biggest mystery of all—their disappearance. Even scientists can't agree on a single theory. See whether your family can offer some insights into the puzzle during a dinner time discussion. Ask:

What really *happened to the dinosaurs?*

Fifty Questions

Subject: Family Circle
Preparation: None

Making compromises is often one of the most difficult things for kids of any age to do. Here's a dinner table activity that can help your children see the opportunities for negotiating, rather than simply demanding.

Pose the following situation: On a particular evening, one group of family members wants to eat at home, while another wants to go to a restaurant. What can they do to resolve the "gridlock?" There are many possibilities. Everyone might agree to eat take out food at home, or everyone could cook in and have dessert out afterwards (or vice versa). Finally, everyone could eat the meal at home, and go out another night.

Ask the people in your family to offer their solutions and opinions, and then try to resolve other situations such as people in conflict about: going to the movies vs. going to a concert; taking a hike in the country or taking a drive; going shopping or visiting a museum; or listening to rock or jazz while in the car.

Perhaps your family has a career awaiting it in the professional negotiating field!

Family Senate

Subject: 'Readin', 'Writin', 'Rithmetic

Preparation: None

Here's a word game that will be a definite test of everyone's spelling skills and vocabulary. You might be surprised at your children's creativity with both!

No paper is necessary for this dinner-time word game, but you can bring a dictionary to the table to check spelling and authenticity. (Unless of course you're going to change the rules and allow creative spelling rendentions—which may be a different game entirely!)

To play Ghost, take turns saying a letter out loud. With each added letter, you must be contributing to a real word that you have in mind—though you haven't shared it with anyone else. It gets tricky as you think of one word and then another to keep the game going. The object: to avoid being the person who says the letter that completes the word.

How about: D-I-N-N-E-R!

Subject: Friendship

Preparation: None

Is it better to give or to receive? Your family can debate the question before holidays, birthdays, and other occasions when gifts are given.

Giving

Giving makes us feel better than receiving. When we give presents, we're showing people how much we care about them. Giving also makes people happy; it lets us share things we have with others. And that's the best feeling there is.

Great Debates

Receiving

Getting presents is much more fun than giving them. We all like to be surprised—to get a box, unwrap it, and find out what's inside. Anyone who says that they'd rather give than receive isn't being honest.

Subject: Politics
Preparation: None

Imagine if everyone in the world spoke one language. The world would be a better place if we could all understand each other, right? See whether your family speaks the same language when you discuss this topic:

One Language
The trouble with this world is that we speak too many languages. No one understands anyone else, and we end up fighting. If everyone spoke the same language, we would stop having wars, and the world would be a happy place.

Great Debates

Many Tongues
Variety is the spice of life, and different languages add flavor to the world. If everyone were the same, we'd have little to learn from one another. We'd be bored with each other pretty quickly. We should celebrate all of our differences, including the way we look, the way we dress, and the way we speak.

Subject: Food
Preparation: None

How's your memory? This game is sure to test your ability to keep up with your kids.

The first person begins by saying, "I'm going on a trip and I'm going to take . . ." then names something, like ". . . my favorite cup." The next person says, "I'm going on a trip and I'm going to take my favorite cup and toothbrush"—repeating the first person's choice and adding something else. The next person names something else and also lists the cup, toothbrush, and teddy bear. The round continues and is over when someone leaves something out.

A variation of this activity is to see who can remember the list backwards or think up the zaniest object. Just why would you want to take along your eggbeater and vacuum cleaner?

Game Time

105 The Golden Rule

Subject: Ethics
Preparation: None

Wise words to ponder:

Do unto others as you would have others do unto you.

Start a great dinner table discussion by asking:

1. Do people you know usually treat others the way they want to be treated themselves?

2. Can you think of a time when, if people had followed the Golden Rule, things would have had a happier ending?

3. How can we convince others to follow the Golden Rule?

4. How would the world be different if everyone followed the Golden Rule?

The Gold Rush 106

Subject: Money Matters
Preparation: None

Wise words to ponder:

All that glitters is not gold.

Start a great dinner table discussion by asking:

1. Can you think of any toy or game that looked great in the picture on the box but turned out to be a disappointment later on?

2. How can you distinguish between the way something looks on the outside and its real value?

3. Is the biggest present with the fanciest wrappings always the best gift?

4. Can fancy clothes or jewelry make someone a better person?

107 A Good Heart

Subject: Ethics
Preparation: None

Wise words to ponder:

A good heart is better than all the heads in the world.

Start a great dinner table discussion by asking:

1. Is it a good idea to do something just because it "feels" like the right thing to do?

2. How about the opposite—do you ever feel like doing something and then "think" yourself out of it?

3. Can you think of good reasons to make decisions from the heart? How about from the head?

4. Would the world be a different place if people all acted from their hearts instead of their heads?

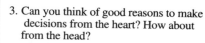

Great Thoughts

Good Listening 108

Subject: Singalong
Preparation: None

Here's a dilemma that you and your family might never face . . . but it's always best to be prepared.

Let's say that you were all stranded on a deserted island. You happened to have brought along a solar-powered tape deck and three cassettes apiece. No one packed any books or toys; the cassettes will be your only source of entertainment. Have your family take turns answering the following questions:

Which three tapes would you bring along, and why? Which tapes that you didn't take would you miss the most?

Let's say your whole family could only bring a *total* of three tapes, and family members disagreed on which tapes to bring to the island. It's up to you, however, to decide which cassettes make the journey. Is there a fair way to make a selection?

Finally, if the cassette player suddenly broke and no one could fix it, what would you do for entertainment? While you're working on it, we'll send out a search party!

Shipwrecked

109 Good Morning!

Fifty Questions

Subject: Self and Emotions
Preparation: None

Who hasn't felt as if he or she got out of the wrong side of the bed on a morning or two? Perhaps your family has some tips on what to do to reverse the mood. This table talk question is sure to evoke some inspiring answers:

What's the best way to make yourself feel happy when you start off your day (even if you're feeling a bit blue)?

Great American Novel 110

Subject: Arts and Media
Preparation: None

Do you have a budding author in your midst? Or at least some avid readers? Whether you do or not, you are bound to get your family's creative flow going with this dinnertime challenge. Try posing the following:

If you could write any book, what would it be about?

Fifty Questions

111 Great Grammar

Subject: Readin', Writin', 'Rithmetic
Preparation: None

Believe it or not, around the dinnertable, grammar can get the enthusiasm it deserves!

After dinner, choose someone (a parent or older child) to conduct a grammar lesson. This "teacher" secretly thinks of a sentence (for instance, "They eat dinner."), and assigns each person a role in the sentence—the verb (eat), subject (they), object (dinner), and punctuation (period). Then, the "parts of speech" verbally arrange the sentence properly, or they could even line up in order, if there are enough participants. Does each player know where he or she goes in the sentence? If this is too easy, then add some additional elements, such as an adjective, adverb, or quotation marks.

Play School

Alternatively, you might want to assign everyone the task of making flash cards before dinner, with each person creating several cards for his or her assigned part of speech, along with some punctuation marks. Then bring the flash cards to the table for a sentence-designing contest. That way, your family can actually see what they're saying!

Grownups Only 112

Subject: Family Circle
Preparation: None

Grownups often look back wistfully on their childhoods; children are often in a great hurry to be more grownup. What's the difference between being an adult and being a child? Have your family share their answers to the following question at the dinner table:

What are some things that grownups get to do that kids don't, and is that fair?

Fifty Questions

113 Guess That Recipe

Subject: Food

Preparation: None

Family Book Works

Sugar and spice, and everything nice. That is what . . . just about anything is made of!

Flip through a cookbook and stop when you find a recipe familiar to everyone. Read the list of ingredients and see who can figure out what you're "cooking." Take turns selecting the recipes and reading the ingredients aloud.

You can also play "guess what's missing," reading all but the most crucial ingredients of a recipe. See who can be the first to figure out, for example, that the ginger is missing from the gingerbread, the meat has been left out of the meatloaf, or that the strawberry pudding contains everything except the strawberries.

Another cookbook game entails reading off a recipe and then having people substitute zany ingredients and cooking steps. Then, they can suggest mouth-watering names for the exotic cuisine. For instance, ingredients that were intended for chocolate chip cookies can find new life as . . . Meatballs Cho-colat . . . Choco-Cheese Soufflé . . . or Fettucini Alchoco (which is delicious when made with fresh peach pit pasta).

Hey—doesn't all this sound like a recipe for fun?

114 Guess the History

Subject: Self and Emotions

Preparation: Find a special object

Soapbox

One thing is for sure: There are some things that you can't put a price on. Their worth lies in what they mean to you.

Have your family take turns showing "mystery" objects. These can be familiar things, like movie ticket stubs or hair ribbons, or more exotic things, like a pet rock or plastic dinosaur. Other family members then take turns guessing the object's history, where and when it was acquired, why it's significant, and so on. Then see whose version comes closest to the real thing. (No fair guessing if you already know the object and its story!)

Alternatively, have a family "show and tell" night with a theme—say, souvenirs of trips or homemade crafts. If you can't find exactly the treasure you're looking for, you can draw it instead.

See how much fun it can be to rediscover old treasures—and share them with your family.

115 Ham It Up

Subject: Arts and Media
Preparation: None

You don't have to live in the big city to experience the thrill of the stage. You can turn your home into a theater, with your family as the featured players, anytime you're all sitting at the table.

First, choose a story that you all know. Any fairy tale, book, or movie will do. Assign a role to each person, and improvise. Or, choose interesting characters to portray, and make up a story as you go along. As you eat, see what situations you find yourselves in, how you interact with each other, and how you handle yourselves.

You can also take turns inventing situations and have family members play their own persona. For example, your family can take an expedition to a rainforest and improvise what happens to them when they arrive.

There's no limit to the plays that your ensemble can stage. So, gather your actors, turn down the houselights, and—curtain!

Dinner Theater

Hands Up 116

Subject: Books and Literature
Preparation: Collect puppeteering materials

Here's a way for your family to let their fingers do the walking . . . and the talking.

Before dinner, make puppets out of small paper bags, socks, mittens, or gloves. For decorations, glue or sew on bits of yarn and buttons, or draw the features using tempera paint, non-toxic markers, or old lipsticks.

Creating your puppets is half the fun; the other is using your puppets to stage your own plays. Use one hand to let your puppets "act" while you eat with the other hand. Your puppets can be the characters in a story that everyone knows, or you can build your own plots; for instance, a sock puppet can face a crisis when somebody decides to launder it, or a pair of glove puppets might go shopping for the perfect thimble-hat to wear to a wedding. With clever costume changes, you can even have the same puppet play more than one role in a show.

For versatility and sheer fun, dinnertime plays with homemade puppets are the popular winners—hands down.

Dinner Theater

117 Hang Onto It?

Subject: Current Events

Preparation: None

Is it all right to throw away recyclable things? Here are some ideas for starting a table talk debate over the matter.

Waste Is Part of Life

Although recycling everything would be ideal, it isn't always possible. Many communities don't support recycling. If there's no recycling in your community, there's nothing you can do as an individual.

Use and Re-use

Even if your community doesn't have a recycling program, there are still things you can do. If you really don't need something, or it's packaged in a wasteful way, then don't buy it! Also, try to find new uses for old things and their packaging as much as possible.

---

118 Headliners

Subject: Current Events

Preparation: Minimal

Gazette Games

A good newspaper headline tells you all you need to know about what's in an article, right? Here's how you and your family can find out how often—or how rarely—the real story is what it seems to be.

Have someone choose an interesting headline from any section of the newspaper—don't forget community news, food, and sports—and read it aloud. Then, take turns guessing what the article is about. (Remember that every article should answer the questions who, what, where, when, and why.) Compare your family's version of the story with the original. How close did you come to guessing the facts?

Alternatively, read an article aloud and see whether your family can invent a good headline for it. Maybe you can improve on the original, or invent one that's wittier, zanier, or more revealing.

Practice sniffing out truths and writing clever headlines. Then, see how it feels to be a Woodward or a Bernstein!

Subject: Family Circle
Preparation: None

It's not only fun to receive recognition for your accomplishments—it's great to recognize others' achievements as well. Here's a chance to show family members how much you admire their accomplishments.

During dinner, poll family members to find out their most recent achievements—maybe it's receiving a good grade on a difficult test, setting a new personal sports record, or making a new work of art. Then have the family think of ways to commemorate the achievements. For instance, you might make certificates of merit for each other that read something like, "Congratulations to Audrey for learning to ride a bicycle with training wheels." (You can use colored paper, crayons, glitter, and glue to make the certificates.) Or, perhaps you can throw an impromptu "after-dinner family celebration party," complete with decorations, games, and your favorite treats, to congratulate everyone at once. Once your agenda is set and the dinner table is cleared, get ready to carry out the plan!

Family Communications

Subject: Self and Emotions
Preparation: None

Wise words to ponder:

Every cloud has a silver lining.

1. Can you think of a time when something seemed bad . . . but a good thing came out of it?

2. Do you believe things usually turn out for the best?

3. What can you tell someone who is sad to help him or her believe that things will turn out okay?

Great Thoughts

Subject: Just for Fun
Preparation: None

Game Time

Even beginning readers will enjoy finding words within words at this dinner table activity—(which is perfect, by the way, any time there's a long wait for dessert).

For this *Table Talk!* game, get ready to think up some good long words. (A dictionary is helpful, of course, but optional.)

The purpose: to see how many smaller words you can form by using some of the letters of longer words. Write the "source" word on a big sheet of paper that everyone can see over dinner, and find out who can use the source to form the most interesting small words. Within orbiculate, for instance, are the words: or, orb, rile, rail, bile, bail, bite, it, ire, cute, core, clue, club, cite, late, lace, lice, lore, lure, ate, are, crate, and boat (and more)! It gets tricky as you start moving letters around—that's why paper and pencil is helpful. (By the way, orbiculate means to encircle.)

Have family members take turns thinking up words. Of course, it will get tougher as most of the words are found. The last one to find a word becomes the hidden word champion of the evening.

Subject: Money Matters
Preparation: None

Some people are disturbed that stores begin promoting Christmas almost immediately following Halloween. Should they be required to wait until December? Here are some ideas for starting a *Table Talk!* debate over the matter.

Great Debates

Business Is Business

Christmas is the best season for retailers; many of them make nearly their whole year's worth of sales during the months right before the holidays. It wouldn't be fair to tell them they couldn't make the most of it. If people don't want to take part in the shopping, no one is forcing them.

Christmas Is Too Commercial

The spirit of Christmas has been nearly ruined by all the commercialization—especially by stores that begin promoting holiday items and decorations too early. There ought to be a law to hold off on promotions at least until Thanksgiving.

Subject: Family Circle
Preparation: None

What does your family think about children who come home from school to an empty house? More and more, mothers and fathers are working full-time, and there's no parent at home after school. Is this alright? Here are some ideas for starting a table talk debate over the matter.

Kids Are Okay at Home

Kids should be able to take care of themselves when no one else is home. The fact is, many parents don't choose to work—they need the money. And most parents make sure their children know how to deal with problems and emergencies that might arise before they leave them home alone.

Kids Need Supervision

Leaving kids home alone, no matter what their ages, is not a good idea. Kids can't handle emergency situations without panicking. If parents need to be out, they should find alternative supervision—by hiring a babysitter or sending the children to someone else's home.

Great Debates

Subject: Readin', Writin', 'Rithmetic
Preparation: None

Is it okay for parents to help out regularly with homework assignments, particularly if it's something they know a lot about? Here are some ideas for starting a *Table Talk!* debate over the matter.

The More Help the Better

The purpose of homework is to learn something—and it shouldn't matter how the learning is done. If parents know something about the assignment or can help figure it out, then they should pitch in. And, if you're stuck on some homework, anybody and everybody should be able to give you some help.

Keep Parents Out of It

The purpose of homework is to learn how to work through problems on your own. If you can't figure something out right away, you should rely on your own ideas to try to solve the problem. Using parents to help is cheating.

Great Debates

Subject: Ethics
Preparation: None

Wise words to ponder:

Honesty is the best policy.

Start a great dinner table discussion by asking:

1. Is there ever a "good" reason to be dishonest?

2. Is it ok to be dishonest if you know you won't get caught?

3. What about when being honest is going to get somebody you care about into trouble?

4. What should you do if you find out that a friend or relative has been dishonest?

Great Thoughts

Subject: Special Days
Preparation: Make a ballot box

Why not set aside a special night to honor some of the best days of the year—holidays?

Have your family nominate their picks for the following categories (you can start the process by offering three or four candidates for each): Single Best Day of the Year, Neatest Holiday Custom, Most Succulent Holiday Meal, Most Important Holiday, Best Idea for a New Holiday, Holiday from Another Culture That You Most Want to Learn More About, and Most Memorable Family Holiday Celebration.

Then have your family write down the categories and their choices on slips of paper and put the slips into the dinner table ballot box. Have someone sort and count the votes and then announce the winners.

Wouldn't you be surprised to find out that the best day of the year, by popular vote, is Mom and Dad's Anniversary?

Cast Your Vote

Subject: Just for Fun
Preparation: Clip pictures from newspapers or magazines

Have you have played the old "telephone" game in which people pass along a message? The final version is usually pretty garbled. Here's a visual variation.

Before dinner, clip some appropriate pictures from newspapers or magazines, leaving off the caption. Then, ask one family member to close his or her eyes while you very briefly hold up a photo. Each person then takes turns whispering to the person whose eyes were closed the nature of the photograph. Whoever conveyed the most accurate account gets to select the next photograph for viewing.

You can vary the difficulty by changing the amount of time you let people see the photograph—increase it for younger children, keep it to a minimum for eagle-eyed older kids. You can also cover up a portion of a picture, and briefly reveal it during the viewing.

For the ultimate challenge, show several pictures at the same time. Can your family members keep them all straight? You'll no doubt get some interesting descriptions as people combine the subject matters!

Gazette Games

Subject: Self and Emotions
Preparation: None

Does it matter how people look? Some people think they can tell a lot about a person by the way he or she appears. Others say that the only way to find out about someone is to get to know the person. Here are some ideas for framing a table talk debate on the subject.

Looks Are What Counts

In this world, how a person looks *does* matter. People who care about themselves are neater, dress better, smile more, and look better. Good-looking people have the most friends, get the best jobs, and live in the biggest houses.

What's on the Inside Counts

Everyone is special, and you can only learn about someone by talking to him or her. It's more important to be a considerate and generous person than to look good.

Great Debates

Subject: Politics
Preparation: Clip newspaper article

How would you like to share your dinner table with the president or some other bigwig from the pages of the newspaper? Clip a newspaper article about a political figure. After dinner, read the article aloud, or summarize it, then ask people to step into the politician's shoes. For example, let's say that the article describes the president's budget proposal. Ask how each person would spend the government's money for education, defense, health, and other programs (children can simply say "more" or "less" rather than give dollar figures, or rank choices in order of their importance).

You can also ask participants to create their own budget categories—this is sure to result in some surprises. (We were astonished to learn that President Noah Bennett's biggest line item for the next fiscal year would be unlimited funds for the manufacture of toy dinosaurs and Fig Newton subsidies).

This activity can cover the waterfront, from the serious—decisions about war, drugs, housing, etc.—to the purely whimsical—like special holidays that your future Fearless Leader would declare.

Subject: Family Circle
Preparation: None

Are people allowed to fib under certain circumstances? Here's an interesting dinner table question to ask your family:

If a family member or close friend asks whether or not you like what he or she is wearing, should you always say what you really think?

Fifty Questions

131 Imagine No Rules

Subject: Law and Justice
Preparation: None

Do parents really need to set limits for their children? Your family can debate the pros and cons of having rules—and the consequences of breaking them—at the sound of the gavel.

Crime and Punishment

Imagine if kids were allowed to do anything they wanted to do? Grownups have to set limits, because otherwise kids would get hurt. If grownups let kids break the rules, then they would be irresponsible and uncaring.

The Sky's the Limit

It's not fair for grownups to tell kids what to do. Kids should do what they want and learn from their own mistakes. If you just do what you're told, you never learn how to think for yourself.

Great Debates

I'm Thinking Of . . . 132

Subject: Just for Fun
Preparation: None

This activity requires only your imaginations and a variety of objects within view of the dinner table. Each participant in this guessing game tries to outwit other family members.

The first person says, "I'm thinking of something [a color]." Everyone then looks around the room for something that color, and tries to guess the object. The person can give out additional clues if no one figures it out. Whoever correctly identifies the object gets to select the next item to be guessed.

For older kids, introduce subtler hints, or switch from color, shape and other "forms" to "function": "I'm thinking of something that has numbers and helps us decide whether to wear raincoats." Answer: the telephone—dial the weather!

Game Time

Subject: Zany Stuff

Preparation: None

Twilight Zone

What if a zany scientist accidentally shrank your family, and you were all only a fraction of an inch tall, as in a popular movie?

Let's say that the transformation took place in the house. Have your family take turns describing what the furniture would look like. How would you navigate your way from one end of a room to the other? How would you avoid getting tangled up in the carpet or falling into the cracks in the floor? How might you pick up and use the phone? What other objects might you find helpful?

Now let's say that you went outside to get help. Where would you go? What dangers would you face on the way? Once you arrived, how would you get somebody's attention? And, most difficult, once you've made contact with people, how would you convince them that you were human beings, and not some new kind of life form?

Subject: Self and Emotions

Preparation: None

Wise words to ponder:

A watched pot never boils.

Great Thoughts

1. Can you think of a time when something seemed to take longer than it really did because you were waiting for it to happen?

2. Think of something you did that was so much fun that time seemed to fly. What was it?

3. Is it really possible to make time go faster?

Subject: Just for Fun
Preparation: None

If you've only read books cover to cover, then you've been missing out on something fun that your whole family could be doing with them.

The designated family "scribe" writes the letters of the alphabet in a vertical line. Then someone opens up any book and reads a sentence at random, with the scribe writing the first twenty-six letters of the sentence in a vertical line to the right of the alphabet. Now you have twenty-six sets of two letters each. See whether you can find a famous person, fictional character, or somebody you know who has the initials of each letter pair.

Family Book Works

You can also play the "match game" version. Everybody uses the same letters but writes down only one person who has each set of initials. See how many letter pair "puzzles" you can "solve," then compare answers to find out who has the most matching names.

Does anyone in your family show a talent for telepathy—or just plain good guessing?

Subject: Just for Fun
Preparation: None

Is it real or is it a mirage? You and your family have been lost in the desert for days now, and you're just about out of food and water. Then you see it, a few miles up ahead. Can it be? Yes, it is—an oasis!

This isn't an ordinary oasis, though. There's the usual water and plant life, but even more importantly, there's also anything else that your heart desires! Some of it certainly never existed in any desert before, or anywhere else, except in your imagination. You're close enough now to make out some shapes, colors, and sounds. So have your family take turns describing what they see and hear.

First order of business—what kinds of foods do you see? Fruits and vegetables growing from exotic plants and trees, or a table spread with a feast for your family?

Are there any strange animals? Tall buildings? Toys? Cars? Any people you know, and if so, what are they doing there?

What are the most exciting things *your* family sees?

Shipwrecked

137 In the Light of Day

Subject: Self and Emotions
Preparation: None

Fifty Questions

What scares you the most . . . and how do you make yourself feel braver when you think about it?

A tried-and-true technique for making scary things seem less frightening is to talk about them with your family at the dinner table! Here's a round-table question to get you started:

---

138 In the Wilderness

Subject: Books and Literature
Preparation: None

Shipwrecked

Reading *is* fundamental—especially when it's your only link to civilization.

Imagine that, for failure to pay homage to the king, your family's been exiled to the wilderness for forty years. Food, shelter, and clothing won't be a problem—you can live off the earth easily enough. But enriching your minds and fending off boredom will be the tougher challenges.

Your family members can take three books with them and nothing else. Which books would you choose, if it were up to you to decide? Would you take a chance on books that you hadn't read yet? (What if you did, and it turned out you didn't like them?) Or, would you take textbooks? (Remember, you wouldn't be able to go to school—this might be your only chance to get an education.) Reference books, perhaps? (An atlas would sure come in handy, wouldn't't it, or a book on botany?) What other books might you need?

Forty years is *a very long time*, so make wise choices!

139 In Which Room?

Subject: Geography
Preparation: None

This *Table Talk!* game is sure to test your powers of memory and concentration. And who knows? Next time you're in a strange city, it may just keep you from getting lost!

After dinner, choose someone to verbally "walk" to someplace else in the house, beginning with where you are at the table right now. For instance, someone might say: "I walk out of the kitchen, take my second right, then a sharp left, and then walk straight for two rooms. Where am I?" Have everyone at the table take turns guessing where this person ended up. You could also go step-by-step rather than room-by-room. This way you might end up at the kitchen stove one time and at the kitchen table another time.

A variation of this game, which adds a bit more of a challenge, is to play it "away from home"—that is, to pretend that you're someplace else, such as at a grandparent's house. Now, how well can you remember the route from Grandma's dining room table to her front porch?

Game Time

I Shall Return . . . Maybe 140

Subject: Science and Nature
Preparation: None

It's common knowledge that dinosaurs are extinct—after all, no one has ever seen a living dinosaur roaming around town. Still, your family might enjoy tackling the following dinner table question:

Do you think the dinosaurs may come back some day? If so, explain when and where.

Fifty Questions

141 Is This the Real Life?

Subject: Arts and Media
Preparation: None

Here's a neat way to get a dinner table reality check about what you watch on television. (Or, if you've stopped watching the tube, you can refer to shows you've heard about or that you might remember seeing.) The question to ask is:

Is everything you see on TV true, and when shouldn't you believe what you see on TV?

142 It Takes Patience

Subject: Self and Emotions
Preparation: None

Is waiting a difficulty for your children? If so, they're certainly not alone! Maybe your kids have something to say about patience, after all. Ask them.

See whether the kids at your dinner table can help the grownups learn a thing or two about patience. Pose this question:

When you have to wait for something you do or have to do right now, what are some things you can do to make the waiting easier?

143 I Wish . . .

Subject: Just for Fun
Preparation: None

How much do you know about what your children want for their future? Here is the perfect opportunity to find out.

After dinner, begin a page of wishes in your family album. Choose one person to act as an interviewer, and another to serve as a scribe. Go around the table, and take turns talking about your hopes and plans for the future. What are people's personal aspirations for the short term and long haul? What do they wish for the larger community, the nation, and the world?

Be sure to date this page of Wishes in your Family Album. In another year you can turn back to it and find out what dreams have come true—or how your wishes have changed!

Family Album

Jot This Down 144

Subject: Family Circle
Preparation: None

Who said that everything you commit to writing has to be of earth-shattering importance? Sometimes it can be fun to scribble down a silly observation or a zany statement or two.

At the dinner table, pass out some note paper and colorful pens. Then, have everyone write an open note to the family, saying whatever is on his or her mind. Perhaps you can share a new philosophy (pelicans have large bills but say little of value) or propose a law (every time somebody eats a forkful of mashed potatoes, he or she must follow it with a sip of water). Then you can collect the notes, read them aloud, and decide whether to live by the new wisdom, or to adopt the new rule, for the duration of the meal.

For extra fun, don't sign the notes. As each message is completed, seal it up; then take turns reading the messages aloud. Can you guess who proposed that the family have two helpings of dessert and skip the broccoli tonight?

Family Communications

146 Junior Moms and Dads

Subject: Law and Justice

Preparation: None

How many times a day do your children challenge the rules in your house? Here's an after-dinner question to pose to your children that may make them think twice next time:

If you were a parent, what are the most important rules you'd make for your own kids, and why would you insist on them?

Fifty Questions

---

145 Jungle Laws

Subject: Law and Justice

Preparation: None

How would your family and friends get along in a world with no laws?

Let's say that you went on safari with some friends (a total of fifty people). You lost your way deep in a jungle and had to spend the next twenty years living together in close quarters.

Before long there were disputes about how to share the work (some people wanted to just lounge around), how to divide the food (so that everyone got enough), and generally how to treat one another. What kind of government would you set up, and how would you keep it in power? If a group of people wanted to pass a law that would be unfair to others, how would you stop them?

Also suppose that first one person, then others, started breaking the laws. How would you restore order? Would you build a jail? Who would mete out punishments?

Wow, it really is a jungle out there!

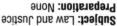

147 Junk Mail

Subject: Zany Stuff
Preparation: Save assorted junk mail

Remember the promise? "Fill out this card and send it to us; no salesperson will call." Well, what if the salesperson *did* call—every time you got an ad in the mail?

Collect a pile of junk mail solicitations and hand one out to each family member. Have participants familiarize themselves with the contents (an adult might brief younger kids), and then take turns role playing a company representative. Offer real or invented information about your organization, make your pitch or plea, and field any questions that the family has.

As a variation, you can pass around a catalog and have each family member choose an item to "sell." Let the salespeople have the floor for three minutes and see whether they can convincingly tout the benefits of their wares. Or, add an element of chance by cutting out some ads, putting them into an envelope or bag, and having family members select their "merchandise."

Would you buy a used car from someone in your family?

Playalong Junk Mail

Jurassic Name Game 148

Subject: Science and Nature
Preparation: None

As dinosaurs continue to gain attention, this activity will encourage everyone to learn a bit more about these strange creatures.

During or after dinner, choose someone to be "it." That person, in turn, selects a specific kind of dinosaur to think about. Now, go around the table asking questions that will help identify the dinosaur. What did it eat? Did it swim or roam around on the ground? Was it gentle-natured or predatory? (A good dinosaur book from the library might be helpful if you don't have one on hand.)

For variety, you can always choose another category of science and nature that is of interest in your family—a category such as planets or stars, birds or butterflies. The possibilities are endless!

Guessing Games

149 Just Because

Subject: Family Circle
Preparation: None

The dinner table can be a great place to talk about important matters, such as current events and politics. It can also be the ideal place to say things that might not shake up the world—but are just nice to say and hear.

Designate a family member as the "honoree" for the evening and then go around the table, having everyone say something positive or make a kind observation about that person. The compliment can be gargantuan (you're the best kid brother on the planet), or humble (you make yummy brownies)—as long as it's sincere. The subject of all the praise must listen silently (no humility is allowed here). The next night it can be another person's turn. (Make sure nobody gets left out.)

The effects of saying and hearing nice things might last for hours—don't be surprised if family members fall asleep smiling!

150 Know-It-Alls

Subject: Self and Emotions
Preparation: None

Twilight Zone

Let's say that your family took part in a wonderful experiment: each of you now had five times the intelligence of Albert Einstein!

Have family members reap the benefits of your newfound brilliance. Take turns playing "Einstein," and have participants bring three of life's greatest questions to you. They can be serious ("What kind of present can I make Grandpa for Father's Day?") or off-the-wall ("How can I grow five inches overnight?").

Perhaps you could designate a category of intellectual prowess for each genius—someone might be in charge of life's big mysteries, another might unravel mathematical riddles, another might invent solutions for everyday nuisances, and so on.

With your combined brainpower, how do you think your lives will change? Will you still remember the "little people" when you win a Nobel Prize for solving the greatest enigma of modern times: what happens to those socks that vanish in the dryer?!

151 Land Before Time

Subject: History
Preparation: None

What if you and your family were riding in a balloon that sailed right through a time warp—and into the land before time?

You manage to get the balloon down safely, only to find that you've arrived on prehistoric Earth. Herbivorous dinosaurs and gargantuan birds come close to inspect you. The sun blazes overhead.

You and your family take a walking tour to get your bearings and to see whether you can find help. What differences, geographical and otherwise, strike you? Do you find any convincing evidence that you're still on Earth?

What kinds of plants and trees are growing? When you wade into the lake to find drinkable water, what kinds of marine life do you encounter?

What other animals do you run into? Do any of them appear to be "talking" to each other? Can you find a way to communicate with them? After all, one of them might be able to help you find some food, or even a way to get home.

Shipwrecked

Land of the Giants 152

Subject: Food
Preparation: None

All kids know they have to eat if they want to grow and build strong bodies. But how much do they really know about the process? Get some insights by tossing out this dinner table question (there's no better place for it!):

If food makes your body bigger, then why don't grownups keep growing until they become giants?

Fifty Questions

Subject: Readin', Writin', Rithmetic
Preparation: None

One way to understand the rest of the world is to speak its language. After dinner, choose someone (a parent or older child) to conduct a foreign language lesson. This "teacher" can then moderate any of the following language activities. For younger kids, stick with learning some simple words or phrases in a number of languages, perhaps simply how to count to ten — "uno, dos, tres, cuatro, cinco, seis, siete, ocho, nueve, diez" (Spanish); and "un, deux, trois, quatre, cinq, six, sept, huit, neuf, dix" (French).

Another way to do this activity is to assign a language to each person a day or so before. That person will then come to the table equipped to teach you the entire alphabet or to share a phrase or two. *Guten abend!*

Subject: Law and Justice
Preparation: Make a ballot box

Some laws are best when you only pretend they exist—for instance, those that result from the following election.

Have your family nominate impossible award-winning homegrown laws such as: "Wildest Pizza Law" (perhaps on Tuesdays, everyone eats pizza with a spoon), "The Most Difficult to Consistently Uphold Law" (such as the one that mandates clapping before you speak), or "The Most Outrageous Dress Law" (everyone has to wear something from a famous children's story during dinner).

Have family members write down their choices, and put their votes into the dinner table ballot box. Tabulate the scores, and announce the prize winners.

What's the zaniest that your family has devised?

Cast Your Vote

Subject: Science and Nature
Preparation: None

The dramatic changes in the colors of the leaves is one of the best parts of fall. Not only is a little leaf-peeping an opportunity for family fun, there is also a lesson here about seasons and nature.

During this dinner time conversation, discuss the changing of the season: shorter days, cooler weather, and the changing colors of the leaves. You can also have each person set a brightly colored leaf on his or her place setting, and discuss with the family the tree from which the leaf came. Then select someone as scribe and pull out the plan book. Together, put together a list of ways to do some leaf-observing. Is there a nature preserve nearby or a particularly colorful drive? Perhaps there are some fall festivals scheduled that would include a drive in the country. Pick a weekend or two to enjoy the season.

You might plan to bring a collection of leaves home to use in other activities, such as leaf pressings and nature collages. The fun of leaves can continue long after they've dropped off the trees for the season.

What's the Plan?

Subject: Zany Stuff
Preparation: None

Heard any good jokes lately? Gather some of the funniest and create a family joke book that's sure to be a hit with your friends and relatives.

You can have each person contribute jokes, riddles, and one-liners. Or have each person tell a funny story, either real or made up—about something that happened to them, someone they know, or someone they've heard about. Younger children can contribute silly pictures to illustrate the book.

Stuck for ideas? How about telling the plot of a funny book you've read or an unusual dream you've had recently?

When you've finished the writing, design a cover, and come up with a book title. Then, before you staple it, be sure to make copies of your book to send to everyone you know who appreciates a good joke. By the way, how do you know that elephants enjoy traveling? Simple: they always have trunks!

Family Communications

157 Leisure Time

Subject: Just for Fun

Preparation: None

Most of us would like to add some spice to our family recreational routines. This activity will help you do just that. During dinner, begin a discussion about your family's leisure-time activities, and have your "senate" members offer some routine-busting innovations. Instead of taking your regular route to the country next weekend, perhaps you can "shunpike" and find some new scenic roads. ("Shunpiking" is a time-honored New England tradition of finding alternate routes; early settlers who didn't want to pay land owners tolls for crossing their fields to get to major roadways were said to "shun the pikes.") Or, perhaps family members will come up with ideas for occasionally substituting do-it-yourself theater productions for Saturday afternoon movie matinees. Discuss all the proposals, then adapt at least one of each person's ideas to try out later. If you enjoy the change, you might even consider making a habit of breaking old, familiar habits!

158 Let It Be

Subject: Ethics

Preparation: None

Wise words to ponder:

Let bygones be bygones.

Start a great dinner table discussion by asking:

Great Thoughts

1. Remember a time when you and a friend or brother or sister argued, and later forgave each other for "bygones?" How did you feel?

2. Can you think of anything that happened in the past that still makes you angry? Can you talk about it and let bygones be bygones?

3. How would the world be a different place if we always practiced this maxim?

159 Let's Check Our Book

Subject: Readin', Writin', 'Rithmetic
Preparation: None

If your house is anything like ours, your family time can get very limited with school, sports, and social engagements. With a family calendar you'll at least know where you are!

After dinner, poll the family on a good, workable calendar. Do you have a large chalkboard? Or perhaps an erasable message board? Even a large piece of construction paper will do. Homemade "stickers" can be made out of cut-out drawings or magazine pictures. With the current month drawn out day by day, first put down everyone's regular commitments—late office days, meetings, clubs. Then, add special events (use fun stickers here!) like birthdays, holidays, and trips.

If this activity catches on, post the calendar someplace where everyone can add things as they come up or collect ideas for family fun.

Family Communications

Let the Good Times Roll 160

Subject: Just for Fun
Preparation: None

When you think about it, isn't quality time the best gift that family members can give to each other? Have your family take some time at the dinner table to respond to the following question (their answers might well come in handy some rainy day):

What are the three best things families can do together to have fun?

Fifty Questions

Subject: Books and Literature

Preparation: None

Have you ever become so absorbed in what you're reading that you lost track of everything around you? If so, this could happen to you!

Imagine that you and your family were having so much fun at the library on a Friday afternoon that you didn't realize it was closing time—and you were accidentally locked in for the whole weekend! There's an employee lunchroom and a well-stocked refrigerator, so food and drinks won't be a problem. But what will you do until Monday?

Take turns answering the following questions: Where will you sleep? How will you exercise? How might you take advantage of the fact that no one will "shush" you, regardless of how loud you get? How will you systematically make your way through your favorite books, magazines, and tapes?

One bright spot—at least there's no fine that we know of for getting locked inside a library!

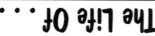

Subject: Self and Emotions

Preparation: None

Everyone has an interesting history to pass down to future generations. Imagine how much a chapter in your Family Album can tell!

Have a designated scribe interview each person at the dinner table, and then write down everybody's full name, nicknames, birthdate, and so on. You might decide to include each person's favorite food, color, number, animal, or anything else that you deem important. Then, with the scribe getting it all down on paper, have family members take turns saying something that characterizes each participant. The record might show that your four-year-old son's greatest traits are his contagious laugh, his extensive knowledge and collection of dinosaurs, and the fact that he always invites his sister and her stuffed bunny on high seas adventures.

You might finish with a short self-description from each "subject," which could read, "I'm four, I'm the youngest child in the family, and what I like best about myself is that . . ." Fill in the blank, and make sure that your descendants get all the facts first-hand!

Family Album

163 Life on Mars

Subject: Zany Stuff
Preparation: None

We have temporarily taken over control of your dining room. There's no need to adjust the lighting or flip the pages of this book. You're in the outer limits of your imagination.

You've just been transformed into a being from another planet. Your family is meeting you for the first time, so introduce yourself. Tell them your name and describe what you really look and sound like (earthlings will only be able to see and hear you in human terms). Describe your home planet and tell what a typical day is like. Tell how you got to Earth, and answer any other questions that the earthlings have.

Now that everyone has been properly introduced, conduct an intergalactic council. See whether you can resolve interplanetary disputes, formulate treaties, devise strategies for cooperative exploration, etc.

You might discover that your dining room is, in fact, the final frontier!

Soapbox

Like a Lion 164

Subject: Self and Emotions
Preparation: None

It's a lot of fun to act out a character role—but how about taking on the persona of an animal? You may learn a lot about your family by asking them the following dinner table question:

If you could be an animal, which one would you most like to be . . . which would you least like to be . . . and why?

Fifty Questions

Subject: Neighborhood Awareness

Preparation: None

How would you like to make a positive difference in your community? If you and your family put your heads together, perhaps you can find a way to make a significant contribution.

During dinner, have a family discussion about some things that seem to be lacking in your neighborhood. Maybe the park or a public garden needs tending, or people are needed to help with a recycling program. Focus on one problem at a time, discuss it in detail, and come up with a plan of family action. You can also use the neighborhood newspaper for some ideas.

Perhaps your family will make time to work on several community projects over a period of time (say, one project a week for a month). That way, everybody's concerns can be addressed. Remember, if your family is part of the solution, then you won't be part of the problem!

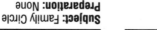

Subject: Family Circle

Preparation: None

Family Senate

Sometimes it takes family encouragement and time to learn new things. Here's a dinner table activity that puts learning on the top of the list.

During dinner, discuss the kinds of things each family member would like to learn, and how the rest of the family can help. Perhaps someone would like to improve his or her baseball game—can the other family members take turns pitching balls? Perhaps mom or dad would really like to take a cooking class two evenings a week at the adult education center—can the rest of the family figure out ways to get the evening cleanup chores done on their own? Or perhaps someone really wants to visit a certain museum for a regular weekend course—can everyone else fit the course in the family's activities for the coming month?

Go around the table and take suggestions for how people can help, with your scribe jotting down the solutions. With a little cooperation and compromising, everyone should be able to do the learning activities he or she wants.

So, what would *you* really like to learn?

Subject: Science and Nature
Preparation: None

Many of us would like to "save the Earth," but we don't know where to start. Well, our idea is this: start right at the dinner table.

During dinner, open up the table for discussion about the way we treat Planet Earth—with pollution and waste topping the list. Then go around the table for ideas for policies to create a "green" home. Suggestions: maximizing the family's recycling resources by putting someone in charge of reusing on a weekly or monthly basis, and turning lights off when a room is empty and the heat down when everyone goes to bed.

Next, go around the table for input on each of the proposals. Will people follow through? Then, take a vote on each before you post your new family policy in a prominent place. You might find that, contrary to what the frog said, it's actually pretty easy—and fun—to be green!

Family Senate

Subject: Self and Emotions
Preparation: None

Some people say that "love is all you need"—and we think there's a lot of truth to that. So, can your family come to an agreement on the following dinner table questions:

How do you know when someone loves you, and what's the best way to show your friends and family that you love them?

Fifty Questions

Subject: Just for Fun

Preparation: None

Shipwrecked

W here's that extra set of keys when you need them? Imagine that you and your family have accidentally locked yourselves in the garage (or, if you don't have a garage, perhaps the family room, attic, etc.). There's no telling when someone will notice that you're missing and come to rescue you. You have two choices: you can either make the best of it or try to "bust out."

Can you figure out how you and your family might entertain yourselves using whatever you could find, make, or imagine? Perhaps you could go for a pretend car ride, use a box of old clothing to put on a play, or find a way to get that tricycle to fly. What else might you do to pass the time?

Let's say it's almost dinnertime now, and you're still locked in. Perhaps, if you and your family put your heads together, you can find a way out. Are there any tools lying around? Or, could you make your own using whatever materials you might find?

With your family's ingenuity, maybe you can solve this locked-door mystery after all!

Subject: Self and Emotions

Preparation: None

Could you be eating in the company of the next Dear Abby or Ann Landers? Here's a chance to match wits with the famous advice gurus.

Have someone flip to an advice column in the newspaper and bring it to the table. (You'll probably want to screen it in advance.) After dinner, toss out an appropriate question from the column and go around the table, having everyone give his or her solution to the problem. See whether your family can reach a consensus. Then, read aloud the answer in the newspaper. Did your family come up with any insights that the columnist missed? Alternatively, have each family member "write a letter" about pressing problems and take turns offering solutions. Or, have participants write down their answers. One person reads them all, and everyone tries to match each gem of wisdom with the person who wrote it.

You're likely to find some of the most creative approaches to life's challenges right at your own dinner table. Abby and Ann, move over!

Gazette Games

171 The Long Way Down

Subject: Family Circle
Preparation: None

Wise words to ponder:

The highest tree has the greatest fall.

Start a great dinner table discussion by asking:

1. Do people generally expect more from "famous" people? Why?

2. Would it be harder to forgive a famous person if he or she did something wrong or something you disagree with?

3. What are the risks of being the "mostest"—having the most and being the best?

Great Thoughts

Love Is . . . 172

Subject: Self and Emotions
Preparation: None

Everyone searches for it and tomes have been written about it. We're talking about love. Ask your family for some insights into this most human of all feelings by asking the people at your table:

Is someone talking about the same feeling when they say, "I love ice cream" as when they say, "I love you"?

Fifty Questions

Subject: Family Circle
Preparation: Collect junk mail

If travel agents, magazine publishers, or timesharing salespeople "visited" your mailbox recently, they most likely left behind a trail of envelopes, stickers, and photographs. See whether your family can use them to create a dinner table post office.

Have each family member turn an empty used envelope (the bigger, the better) into a personal mailbox, complete with a name and decorations.

Then have everyone write letters and postcards using mail leftovers. You can paste "borrowed" letterheads on sheets of paper to create your own stationery, or tape photographs onto reply cards to make postcards. Compose a special message (dinner was great, glad you were here), "address" it (Dad, left side of the table, second chair in, our house, planet Earth), attach a sticker for postage, and "mail" it to the recipient.

After dinner, have your family share the contents of their mailboxes with each other. You can bet they won't find any junk mail this time!

Subject: Self and Emotions
Preparation: None

Great Thoughts

Wise words to ponder:

It is better to be born lucky than rich.

Start a great dinner table discussion by asking:

1. Do you consider yourself a lucky person? If so, what are some lucky things that have happened to you?

2. Is there really such a thing as luck, or is it just the way people look upon the things that happen in their lives?

3. Is it possible for everyone to see themselves as lucky in some way?

Subject: School Matters
Preparation: None

Why do teachers grade schoolwork? Do test scores help kids learn more—or do they only discourage some kids and make them stop trying? When the school bell rings, your family can begin the debate.

We Need Grades
Grades tell kids how much they've learned and whether or not they're keeping up with the others in their class. Without tests, kids wouldn't study and they'd stop learning.

Grades Are Useless

Grades don't show whether kids have learned anything—they just show how good they are at taking tests. Why not eliminate grades and switch to a pass/fail system—anybody who didn't put in enough effort would have to take the course over again? That way teachers would spend more time teaching and less time giving tests, and kids would learn more.

Great Debates

Subject: Sports
Preparation: None

Contrary to some critics' opinions, mimes can be great fun. During dinner, see whether the mimes at your house can conjure up the image of somebody . . . driving a car, riding in an airplane, having fun in a swimming pool, painting a masterpiece, preparing a meal, washing the windows, playing in the snow, building a log cabin, planting a garden, walking on the moon, and grocery shopping—all while seated at the table. Have family members mime these activities, and invent others, singly or as a group. Or, have family members individually pantomime something that they choose (or an activity written up on a piece of paper they've picked out of a bag), while others try to guess what they are miming.

You can also have two mimes "mirror" each other. One person "leads" by moving an arm, leg, fingers, etc., and the other person tries to "follow" each action exactly and smoothly.

Pantomime lets family members see each other in a whole new way. Notice how much you can show one another—without even saying a word!

Dinner Theater

Subject: Friendship

Preparation: None

Perhaps you are thinking of moving across town or even across the country—or perhaps a house on the street has recently been bought by a family with children. Here's how to elicit advice from your family on meeting new friends. At the dinner table, ask:

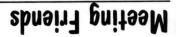

Let's say a new person joins your class or company, or moves into the neighborhood—what's the best way to make friends with him or her?

Subject: Zany Stuff

Preparation: None

Twilight Zone

Let's say that an extraterrestrial craft landed in your backyard. You and the family of extraterrestrials traded places—they became humans and lived on Earth, and you became aliens and went back to live on their planet.

What would your new bodies look like? How tall would you be? What language would you speak? What would your house look like? What kinds of food would you eat? What would you drink? What would you do for fun? Would the younger alien family members go to school? What would they study? Would the older aliens work? What would they do for a living?

Also, what would you like best about your new lifestyle? What would you miss the most about being human? If you had a chance to trade places again with the extraterrestrials living on Earth—would you?

Now, would you and your family be as friendly next time a UFO lands in your backyard?

179 Memory Testers

Subject: Just for Fun
Preparation: None

Here's a game that will test everybody's powers of observation and memory. You may be surprised at the details you never thought you saw before!

After dinner, ask everyone at the table to shut his or her eyes. Then, with each person taking a turn, select a category of objects from the room where you're sitting for players to try to recall. Here's an example. The first person might say, "Things that are green." How many green objects are in the room? How about the curtains, someone's sweater, the napkins? Then, when you run out of green objects, pick another category—say, things that are round. How many round objects are in the room? Mirrors, plates, buttons? (Remember, everyone's eyes are still closed.)

A variation of this game is to play it while having family members imagine they're in another, familiar place. For instance, everyone might think of knick-knacks in a grandparent's house. Now, that's really putting your powers of recall to the test!

Game Time

The Midas Touch 180

Subject: Arts and Media
Preparation: None

What if you and your family were suddenly endowed with the "Midas Touch"—and everything you laid a hand on turned to gold? Have your family discuss the following:

Would you enjoy having the ability to turn everyday objects into a fortune? What kinds of things could you transform into gold without regret (your least favorite foods, perhaps)? What would you do with all your new wealth?

How might having the Midas Touch complicate your life? What would it be like to have to think before you touched anything (and to refrain from hugging family members)? Is there any danger of acquiring too much wealth? What other kinds of problems might arise, and how would you handle them? Do you think you'd really be happier if everything that glittered were gold?

Twilight Zone

Subject: Money Matters
Preparation: None

W ise words to ponder:

Though the emperor be rich, he cannot buy one extra year.

Start a great dinner table discussion by asking:

1. Can you think of two or three important things money can't buy?

2. What about the things money *can* buy—do they measure up to those that can't be purchased?

3. How would the world be different if people focused more on the things that money can't buy instead of on money itself?

Subject: Self and Emotions
Preparation: None

Feelings can get confusing sometimes—especially when we have mixed emotions. Here's an interesting way to explore the issue at the dinner table:

How is it possible that family members and friends can love each other and be angry with each other at the same time?

183 Mousetraps, Etc.

Subject: Just for Fun
Preparation: Clip ads

Advertisements can be wonderful sources for creative fun—and not just for the people who write them. This activity should lead to some pretty creative sessions at your dinner table.

Before dinner, clip a stack of ads from newspapers, magazines, mail order catalogs, and junk mail. Make sure that you have a broad selection of different types of items, ranging from common household goods, such as pots and pans, to high tech stereos and computers,

Select several incongruous ads, such as one for a car, a food processor, and all-weather deck stain, then read off some of the features—air conditioning, purées in seconds, and guaranteed not to fade or peel. What is this mystery product?! Have people name and describe the creation that would combine all of these features into one amazing, new, "must-have" gizmo. (They can also try to guess the correct origins of the features.)

Sound far-fetched? Who knows, you might just create a better mousetrap!

Game Time

Mr. and Ms. Manners 184

Subject: Ethics
Preparation: None

Kids hear it all the time: "Use your manners!" Eventually most give in. But what do kids really think about manners? Find out by asking yours the question:

What are table and other manners, and why do we consider them so important?

Fifty Questions

185 Munching Mandates

Subject: Food

Preparation: None

Here's an activity that will get everyone a bit more involved in the food selections in your house. (Sorry, no promises that they will always eat the right foods!)

During dinner, discuss some of each family member's mealtime likes and dislikes. Perhaps people have different favorites and would like to have them more often.

Once the menu has been agreed upon, have a scribe write it up. Young children can contribute their artwork, so the menu will be as mouthwatering as the actual fare! Make sure the menu indicates who will be the helpers, so each child has the opportunity to participate in making his or her favorite dishes on the coming week's menu.

Can everyone go along with them as fair and reasonable? Then put each of the suggestions up for a vote. By meal's end, your scribe should have new rules to post on the refrigerator door!

186 My Best Friend

Subject: Friendship

Preparation: None

Sometimes we get so attached to our friends that it feels as if we've known them all our lives. Here's a chance to "meet" a friend for the first time, again. This time, though, you'll meet your friend through the eyes of your family.

Choose somebody about whom you know a lot—your best friend or an old family friend. (It's more fun if everyone in your family knows the person.) Then, "introduce" your family to your friend. Describe the person as though your family has never met him or her. Tell what the friend looks like, where he or she is from, how you met, your favorite thing about the person, and what kinds of things you like to do together. Explain why your family should get to know this person—what makes him or her so special?

Find out whether other family members view your friend the same way that you do. Have them paint a word portrait of the same person. See how it's similar to yours and how it's different. Maybe you'll even find a new reason to value your best friend!

Subject: Neighborhood Awareness
Preparation: None

No matter where you live—the city, the country, or a suburb—there's likely to be someplace in the neighborhood that's special to you. Whether you just moved into your community or you've lived there all your life, you've probably discovered that place already.

Have family members take turns telling about their favorite place in the neighborhood. This can be a building, an outdoor spot, or even somewhere in your own house. Tell how you first found it, your favorite memories of the place, and why it's so special to you.

We can travel far and wide, but sometimes the best places of all are right in our own backyards.

Soapbox

My Hero

Subject: Self and Emotions
Preparation: None

Everybody has a hero, whether it's a relative, teacher, actor, sports figure, astronaut, or president. Who are the role models in your family's lives, and what does that tell you about each other's values and goals?

Have everyone tell about the person they most admire, and why. You can either leave the question open-ended or set some parameters. For instance, you can have each person choose a hero who falls into one of the following categories: a celebrity, an older relative, a head of government, a teacher, a sports figure, and a famous inventor.

You can also have each person conjure up his or her ideal person and offer details about this (imaginary) person.

So what kinds of heroes do your kids want to be when they grow up?

Soapbox

Subject: Books and Literature

Preparation: Bring books to table

Our favorite books are a bit like old friends. Even if it's been a while since we've seen them, we can still pick them out of a crowd.

Before dinner, have each person pull a family-pleasing book from the bookshelf, keeping the cover out of sight. Then, over dinner, when it's your turn, read the first line of the book aloud. See who can guess the title of the book. If nobody guesses correctly, you can give a hint, go on to the second line, or try reading a random line from another page.

When somebody correctly guesses the book title, ask about other details. Find out who remembers the names of all the main characters, the plot, setting, and so on.

Once you've rediscovered some of your favorite books, you might be inspired to put some of the best aside for family reading time. It's important that we make an effort to stay in touch with our old friends!

Subject: Books and Literature

Preparation: None

Is there a character from fiction who could use your help getting out of a scrape? A letter of comment or advice in this case could be good practice in problem solving.

Over dinner, have your family choose a fictional character who is in a difficult spot—perhaps Winnie the Pooh, or, for older kids, Tom Sawyer. Discuss the predicament—as well as the book's proposed solution. Does anyone have any better ideas? Pick a character as well as a scribe and compose a family letter of advice.

At this point, you may very well have a revised version of a classic tale on your hands. You might want to re-tell (and perhaps also draw new pictures to illustrate) the tale from the beginning. What new twists and turns develop from your family's advice? Perhaps, in the future, Ebenezer Ⅲ will receive an award of distinction for helping so many needy people!

Take a Letter

191 Name That Animal

Subject: Science and Nature
Preparation: None

Do your kids enjoy talking about animals? Here's a dinner-time activity that will get everyone thinking about their favorites.

Begin by choosing someone at the dinner table to be "it." That person should then bring to mind an animal—the family dog or backyard squirrel or a wild beast from the zoo. Next, go around the table taking turns asking questions to try to identify the animal. Do we see it at the zoo? In our yard? At the park? What does it eat? When does it sleep?

This activity can be adapted for an older child or someone studying animals in school by allowing the guessers to try to outwit the thinker. If guessers ask something about the animals that they can't answer—they lose their turn!

Guessing Games

Name That Tune 192

Subject: Singalong
Preparation: None

Does your family enjoy making music together? Then try this dinner table activity and "clap out" all of your favorite tunes as loudly as you please—since you're at home, volume should be no problem.

Take turns choosing a song that everyone in the family knows and clapping out the rhythm, one note at a time. Then have everyone else guess what the song is. It's a good idea to start with some simple melodies, then step up the challenge. If you live in a houseful of musicians, it won't be long before you try something as complicated as "The Star-Spangled Banner."

A variation of this game is to tap out the tune on each other's back—that way, you can actually feel the rhythm instead of merely hearing it. (This is particularly fun with younger children.) Yet another variation adds an interesting challenge: clap out a note at a time, and see who can guess the tune first. Perhaps the winner can lead the family in singing the song at the dinner table!

Game Time

Subject: Neighborhood Awareness

Preparation: Make a ballot box

Cast Your Vote

Unfortunately, they rarely hand out awards to deserving neighbors. But your family can change all that by holding a "Neighbor Night" at the dinner table.

Have your family nominate some of the people who make your community great (and think of several candidates for each category yourself). Decide who receives the titles: Most Fun to Play With, Most Reliable, Longest Resident, Most Entertaining Neighborhood Newcomer, Most Athletic, Best Gardener, Most Respected Elder, Most Interesting Occupation, and Nicest to Kids. You can even include a special category for Best Pet.

Now have your family discuss the merits of all the candidates (from the above category winners), and hold an election for the ultimate award: Most Valued Neighbor. Tough to choose, isn't it?

Subject: Science and Nature

Preparation: None

Play School

How can we solve large-scale pollution problems? Perhaps your family can offer some ideas for the scientific community and the government.

Choose someone at the dinner table (a parent or older child) to conduct a lesson about an environmental problem—say, ozone depletion, oil spills, or squandering our natural resources. Once the "teacher" has "taught" the lesson, it's up to the family to think of some way to help. Perhaps your family can devise interesting ways to cut down on waste, prevent oil spills, and so on.

If this activity catches on, you may want everyone to do a bit of research on "assigned" topics. Maybe a trip to the library will provide ideas for solving some environmental problems—or a list of organizations that can offer more information and suggestions. Who knows where your dinner table sessions will lead—perhaps your family will find an innovative way to save a rain forest halfway around the world!

Subject: Family Circle
Preparation: None

Is time a limited resource in your household? If so, here's a way that family members can give each other a priceless gift.

During or after dinner, have each person list several things that he or she simply doesn't have enough time to do in a day. Maybe someone wishes he or she had ten minutes more to read the paper. Maybe someone else would like 30 minutes more to practice a musical instrument or favorite sport. Your family "scribe" should take copious notes for the Family Album.

Once everyone has described his or her "time wishes," ask family members to discuss how they can make those wishes come true. Could the youngest kids get their clothes organized or get themselves dressed so mom or dad could have that extra 10 minutes of newspaper-reading time in the morning? Or maybe dinner could be pushed back half an hour on certain days, allowing more time for music or sports practice.

Family Album

True, you can't buy time, but as this activity shows, you can help give it away!

Subject: Family Circle
Preparation: None

Some of us want to stay kids forever. Others can't wait to grow up. Who has more fun, grownups or kids? Talk about it, and see whether you have any Peter Pans in your family.

I Don't Want to Grow Up
It's more fun to be a kid than a grownup. Kids get to play with toys, and they don't have to work because grownups give them everything they need. Kids don't have any real problems or responsibilities. All they do is have fun all day long.

Grownups Have All the Fun
Grownups get to have all the fun. They don't have to follow anybody's rules, and they have the money to buy anything they want. Fun doesn't really begin until you grow up, finish school, and move out on your own.

Great Debates

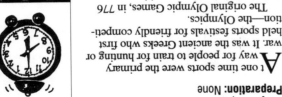

197 Newcomers & Old Hands

Subject: Politics
Preparation: None

Some people argue that the length of time members of Congress serve in Washington is too long, while others believe that long-time members are better equipped to do their job. Here are some ideas for starting a table talk debate over the matter:

Great Debates

Newcomers Bring New Ideas

Electing new people to Congress is a good idea because it brings fresh brainpower and ideas into the government. When people stay in office too long they become more concerned about keeping their jobs and getting reelected than coming up with new solutions to old problems.

Old Hands Hold the Power

If someone is doing a good job in Congress and the people he or she represents want to reelect him or her, they should be free to do so. Experience in running government doesn't come overnight, remember.

---

198 The New Olympic Games

Subject: Sports
Preparation: None

At one time sports were the primary way for people to train for hunting or war. It was the ancient Greeks who first held sports festivals for friendly competition—the Olympics.

The original Olympic Games, in 776 B.C., included such competitions as running, boxing, long-jump, discus, and javelin throwing. During this dinner table travel, imagine that you have been sent to serve on the original Olympic judging committee. Your task: to convince the committee to add some new competitions—in addition to the traditional races—that involve games and materials many years away from invention, such as basketball, hockey, and, most curiously, tobogganing!

Time Travel

199 Next In Line

Subject: Politics
Preparation: None

The vice president's job description is probably one of the nation's better-kept secrets. See whether your family can solve the mystery by asking:

What does the vice president do, and if you don't know for sure, can you take a guess?

Fifty Questions

No-Calorie Menus   200

Subject: Food
Preparation: Collect supermarket circulars

The world's most tempting foods can be found in supermarket circulars, if not always in the aisles.

Have your family cut out a variety of pictures from your local supermarket's advertisements, and see whether they can combine them to create complete, nutritious meals (provide safety scissors for younger kids). Each family member might be assigned a different meal to "cook" (breakfast, lunch, snacktime, dinner), with the whole family working as a team to make sure the day's menu contains enough servings of all the basic food groups.

Family members can also take turns using the pictures to create their own dream meals. How about ice cream pie for the entree, potato chips and onion rings for the vegetables, and a side of whipped cream with chocolate syrup?

Dessert, anyone?

Playalong Junk Mail

202 Not Always Greener

Subject: Self and Emotions

Preparation: None

W ise words to ponder:

Envy accomplishes nothing.

Start a great dinner table discussion by asking:

1. What's the difference between admiring other people's achievements and envying them?

2. What kinds of achievements or things do you envy about other people?

3. When you're feeling envious of someone, what can you do to feel better about yourself?

Great Thoughts

---

201 No Ifs, Ands, or Buts

Subject: Story Making

Preparation: None

D o you believe that great literature can be written by committee? Well, here's a chance to try out the theory—and you might be in for a surprise.

During this dinnertime game, the family gets together to create an original story. Someone begins the tale with one word (say, "Once"). Then, have everyone take turns adding a single word (for instance, "upon," "a," and "time."). The challenge is this: You must tell the whole story without using the words "if," "and," or "but." As you'll discover, this is a lot tougher than it sounds!

You might want to select someone as scribe to write down the plot, or turn on a tape recorder to preserve the tale. See what kind of success you can have creating a family master-piece!

Game Time

Subject: Friendship
Preparation: None

Is there someone in the neighborhood or at school who is always helping out or maybe just brightening up your day? Here's a way to tell the person that he or she is appreciated.

Consider some of the people who you see day after day—it could be the school crossing guard or the neighbor who always says good morning or even a babysitter who is always a lot of fun—and write up a family thank-you letter letting them know just what a difference they've made in your lives. Older children and parents can do the actual writing, while younger children can dictate the letter's contents and work on the paper design or card.

If this activity catches on at your house, you can make it a monthly event. Ask each family member for his or her nominee for the family "Person of the Month" award. Soon, everyone will be thinking about which of his or her neighborhood friends could be the next winner!

Take a Letter

Subject: Self and Emotions
Preparation: None

Wise words to ponder:

The only thing we have to fear is fear itself.

Start a great dinner table discussion by asking:

1. In what ways do people behave differently when they're afraid?

2. What is the first thing you would say to someone who was scared? Why?

3. List one or two things that you are afraid of. Compare your list among the members of your family. Are they the same things?

4. When faced with the scary thing—what do you generally do? And, now that you're thinking about it—is that the best way to respond?

Great Thoughts

Subject: Just for Fun
Preparation: None

Treat your family to a performance of your favorite singers without waiting in long lines, paying outrageous ticket prices, fighting traffic, or walking miles to get from your car to the concert hall. In fact, you can hear the best concert ever—without even leaving your house!

Simply have family members "become" their favorite singers. Choose a song for which the vocalist is famous, and then bring the singer to life.

Alternatively, have your family perform duets or become an entire musical group.

With a little bit of imagination, you can turn your dining room into a great concert hall. What's that? Is it true that Elvis was recently sighted at your house?

Subject: Just for Fun
Preparation: None

Gazette Games

What's the most important part of the newspaper? You and your family probably have different viewpoints, and that's where the fun begins.

Pass a newspaper around the dinner table and have everybody choose a section. (No need to dissect the tabloid—each family member can "claim" a section verbally, then pass the paper to the next participant.) You can select the part of the newspaper that you always read first (perhaps the horoscope), or you can opt for a section you just can't miss (the sports section, maybe). Then, have family members take turns telling why their section is the most important.

So, you say that the weather report is the most informational section in the newspaper, followed by the comics, the food pages, the gossip column, and finally, the headline story? Whatever works for you!

207 Now We're Cooking

Subject: Food
Preparation: None

You might not be able to get your children to help prepare the meals every day, but this activity will get them thinking about all that's involved.

During or after dinner, select someone in the family to be "it." That person imagines something that involves cooking—a food item, the stove, or even cooking words like "teaspoon," "basting," or "blending." Next, take turns going around the table trying to uncover the word in mind. Can you eat it? Raw or cooked? Does it need to be refrigerated? If it's an action, have you ever done this yourself?

One way to adapt this activity for younger children is to limit the choice of items to a food group—something they are familiar with (say, fruit). So, what would you be eating if the description were small, round, red morsels with pits? A bowl of cherries, naturally!

Guessing Games

Now, What's That Again? 208

Subject: Just for Fun
Preparation: None

This dinnertime game promises to be full of surprises. Get ready with your family to "see" things in a whole new way.

To begin, choose someone ("it") to close his or her eyes. Then have family members take turns handing that person objects—say a garlic press or salt shaker—from the kitchen or any other room in the house. The idea is for the player to identify the item merely by touching and handling it (no breakable objects, please!). If he or she doesn't guess correctly, another person hands him or her an object to identify. As soon as the player guesses what the item is, it is someone else's turn to be "it" and close his or her eyes. (You might want to specify the room or the category beforehand to make the game a little easier. Also, when playing with younger children, it might be a good idea to preselect a number of items for safety.)

You can have fun using objects with distinctive textures, such as styrofoam balls, velvet cushions, and cotton balls. Could you identify a marshmallow with your eyes closed?

Game Time

Subject: Self and Emotions

Preparation: None

Wise words to ponder:

The best mirror is an old friend.

Start a great dinner table discussion by asking:

1. Think of your best or oldest friends—what traits do they have that make it easy for you to be their friend?

2. Now think of yourself. What are your traits that make you a worthy companion to your best friend?

3. Ask your family—are the traits you named the same things they think of?

4. Can you think of some reasons others see us differently from the way we see ourselves?

Great Thoughts

Subject: History

Preparation: Look in a book

Here is a chance for your family to prepare a "travelog" through history. Consider coming to dinner dressed for the part, or picking a prominent person from your society to portray. (Or both!)

After assigning research on some ancient civilization, such as the Roman Empire, the Greek Empire, or the Mayans, a day or so before, take turns around the table sharing information about each of these societies. What was their greatest moment? Why should we remember them? How did the people live? Does anything remain from their civilization?

If this activity catches on, choose someone to be scribe and make a list of questions about each of the civilizations. Then you might either do a follow-up report or plan a trip to a nearby museum.

Show and Tell

211 On a Jet Plane

Subject: Just for Fun
Preparation: None

Who hasn't dreamt of being able to soar through the sky like a bird at least once or twice? What if it were possible? Here's a dinner table question that will spark some imaginative answers:

If you could fly, where would you fly to and why?

Fifty Questions

One Nation 212

Subject: Politics
Preparation: None

Would the world be a better place if there were no separate countries, or do nations serve an important purpose? Here are some ideas for starting a table talk debate over the matter:

One Nation United
If the world were one nation, we would all share our resources. There would be no hoarding by one country and starving by another. Of course, we would all agree on laws, which would eliminate war and the suffering that comes with it.

Different but Equal
Different countries make the world an interesting place. Making it all one nation wouldn't necessarily solve the problems— no single country has solved all of its problems. Instead, we would lose the diversity, culture, and beauty of different histories, traditions, and customs.

Great Debates

|

On Mount Olympus

Subject: Books and Literature

Preparation: Look in a book

Here's a chance to share some of the drama from myths and legends. You may want to take a quick trip to the library before embarking on this one.

After "assigning" topics—a choice from Greek, Roman, or Norse mythol-ogy—a day or so before, take turns around the table sharing information about each of these ancient legends. When were they created? Why should we remember them? How did people use them in their lives? Does the story teach us a lesson that still makes sense?

Another way to do this activity is to have people come to dinner dressed as a character from their myths—perhaps they can perform a monologue as well. If nothing else, you'll have a great idea for your next theme party!

Show and Tell

One of a Kind

Subject: Self and Emotions

Preparation: None

There are times when it's hard to feel special and important. Here's a dinner table question that will help your family members remind themselves of their unique qualities even when they're down.

Ask:

What makes you feel special and glad that you're you?

Fifty Questions

Subject: Just for Fun
Preparation: None

Radio stations air commercials plain and fancy throughout the day. Some ads have catchy jingles or sound effects, but many of the best spots simply rely on clever copy and good delivery of the message. See whether your family can create "advertisements" for each other that would make anybody want them as part of their family.

Once you've decided on a theme for the person (or family pet), you'll want to write a script that touts the best things about him or her. Then, after you've assigned roles to your family (announcer, lead actors, supporting players, etc.), you'll want to rehearse so that you'll be ready when it's time to hit the airwaves.

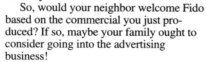

So, would your neighbor welcome Fido based on the commercial you just produced? If so, maybe your family ought to consider going into the advertising business!

Radio Days

Subject: Family Circle
Preparation: None

Everyone likes to receive letters, but did you know that sending letters can be just as much fun when your family does it together?

Take some time to compose a newsy letter to a faraway relative during dinner, or tape ideas while at the table. One person can be designated to write it all down, or you can take turns, passing the letter around after each sentence or paragraph. You might begin the letter with general family news, then create a separate paragraph giving news about each family member until the letter is complete.

Younger children might want to dictate their news for someone else to write down, or they might want to contribute pictures. After the letter is written, have each person sign his or her name at the bottom.

See whether you can encourage relatives to become pen pals with your family, and disprove the popular idea that letter-writing is a lost art.

Family Communications

217 Oral Tradition

Subject: Family Circle
Preparation: None

Soapbox

Here's a neat way to explore old family legends and trace your "roots."

Have each family member pick an older relative, living or deceased, and relate the highlights of that person's life. If you can, include histories of the relatives who emigrated to the United States. Where did they come from, when and how did they get here, and why did they leave home? What was life like when they first arrived?

In light of what you've learned about your relatives, it's time to reevaluate the old saying that the apple doesn't fall far from the tree. Is it true for your family?

218 Our National Treasures

Subject: Current Events
Preparation: None

What if we had a program of "living national treasures"—artists, writers, poets, scholars, thinkers, and others who make great contributions to our society. Who would your family nominate for such an award?

During or after dinner, ask people to create categories that they think would be important for living treasures. For instance, how about: Most Influential Teacher, Most Widely-Followed Musician, Best Authors, Most Courageous Citizen, and Most Dedicated Politicians. Then have people write down their nominations for each category and cast their votes. Draw the nominations, and ask each person to explain why his or her nominees would qualify.

Younger children will probably nominate people in their own immediate sphere of experience, or even storybook characters, while older kids should be encouraged to suggest people who have been in the news or who they've been studying in their classrooms.

You may be surprised to learn your kids' special picks!

Cast Your Vote

Subject: Money Matters
Preparation: None

It would be nice if we could take care of everyone in the world—make sure that everyone had a place to live, that no one went to bed hungry, and that everyone got an education—but we can't help everyone at the same time. What's the most important way for you to help others?

Helping Begins at Home
We should take care of ourselves first, then the people in our neighborhood, then the people in our state, and then those in other parts of the country. Only after that can we begin to worry about the rest of the world.

Helping Begins Where It's Needed
Our priority should be to help those who need help the most. If there are people starving, we should feed them no matter where they live. We can't let people suffer when we could help them. Charity may begin at home, but it doesn't end there.

Great Debates

Subject: Science and Nature
Preparation: None

Here's an activity that is sure to spark the explorer in all of us. Is there anyone who hasn't wanted to play some part at "mission control?"

After dinner, choose a parent or older child to conduct a space mission. Everyone else at the table then becomes a member of the "fleet." The "commander" is in charge of creating some situations. Say you have been drawn suddenly into orbit around a strange, huge planet—winds seem to swirl in both directions and a bright ring of ice particles seems to hang around it. Where are you? (Saturn) Can anyone report on the condition of the surface? Or say instead that you have come to a landing on a bleak, dry, grayish place with some mountainous highlands in the distance. Where are you? (The moon)

Another way to do this activity, especially for younger kids, is to create some drawings or collages from materials culled from old magazines. What do we imagine life is like on other planets?

Play School

Subject: Science and Nature
Preparation: None

Fifty Questions

O f course, no one knows the answers to all life's big questions—but it can sure be fun to guess! See how your family members, especially young children, respond to the following dinner table puzzle:

Where does the sky end?

Subject: Family Circle
Preparation: None

Great Debates

I s it okay for parents to interfere when they see their kids making a mistake, or should they stand back and let their kids learn on their own? Here are some ideas for starting a table talk debate over the matter:

Kids Need a Guiding Hand
Whenever parents see their children making a mistake, they should step in, sit them down, and explain what the mistake involves. Kids can benefit from their parents' experience and wisdom.

Experience Is the Best Teacher
Parents cannot solve all of their children's problems—some things just have to be learned by doing. Besides, not everyone agrees on which things are mistakes.

Subject: Sports
Preparation: None

Would Little League be more fun if kids played by themselves and there were no grownups involved? Here are some ideas for starting a table talk debate over the matter:

Keep 'Em Involved
We need parents! Little League is a lot more fun when we have grownups helping us practice, play hard, and stick to the rules. Parents can help us play ball the right way—and they can make sure that everybody gets to play.

Keep 'Em Off the Field
Grownups take all the fun out of kids' sports. They want their kids to win, so they push too hard. They can be poor losers when their kids' teams lose, too. Kids have the most fun when everyone enjoys the game and nobody really keeps score.

Great Debates

Subject: Family Circle
Preparation: None

If a kid arrives at a friend's house and discovers that some of the other children are doing things that could get them in trouble, what's the right thing to do—should he or she leave or stay? Here are some ideas for starting a table talk debate.

Just Enjoy It
When you go to a friend's house, you are there to have a good time. If there are things going on that you don't like, then you should just ignore them. When you're not having fun anymore, then you should leave. But it's not your responsibility to make sure everyone's doing what you would do at all times.

Not Right Means Just That
If a friend's parents aren't home, you have a responsibility to check things out before you decide to stay. If there is a possibility that someone could get hurt, you should return home and tell your parents.

Great Debates

225 Pass It On

Subject: School Matters
Preparation: None

We all learn something new every day, even though we're usually unaware of the learning process. This activity heightens your awareness of your day-to-day learning process and allows you to pass on your knowledge.

For kids, it's easy to pinpoint a newly learned fact, concept, or theory. All they have to do is think back to the school day (although, as we all know, younger children are often reluctant to report on what they did in school; coax gently).

You might have to pause for a moment and recollect your day. What did you hear on the radio? Read in the paper or book? Maybe you learned about a faraway place, or learned a new word. Did you pick up something from a conversation with a friend, colleague, or coworker? The more you focus on what you learn in a day, the easier it will get to remember.

So, what was your lesson for today?

226 Past Presidents

Subject: History
Preparation: Look in a book

Parents often forget to share pieces of their own history with their children.

In this dinnertime "assignment" activity, choosing a president you remember is a good opportunity to do just that.

After "assigning" a family topic—a past president—a day or so before, take turns sharing information about him, including the way the country was at the time he grew up or served in office, what he is remembered for, things he accomplished, and so on. Then, open up the talk to your own personal memories of this president—the kind of things you don't get from reading history books. Did anyone ever hear him speak in person, or see him during a visit to your state?

Hail to the Chief!

227 Past Vacations

Subject: Family Circle
Preparation: None

Before you lose track of all the fascinating places you've been, get them down on paper.

Over dinner, have everyone recall the memorable trips you've taken together to record in your family album. You can begin with the most outstanding vacations, or you can describe the most recent vacation and then work your way back. You could even include Mom and Dad's honeymoon, or any vacations they remember taking when they were children! Summarize each vacation in a sentence or two (that canyon was fun to explore, but I wouldn't want to live there!), then add details: the date of the trip, the hotels, motels, or campgrounds where you stayed, the restaurants you ate at, how the weather was, and what you did and saw.

"Word" pictures can capture all the fun times that your family photographer might have overlooked, underexposed, or shot out of focus!

Family Album

People Polls 228

Subject: Politics
Preparation: None

While polls on every subject are gaining in popularity, you and your kids may not yet have been part of an official survey. But you can still make sure that your opinions are heard when you conduct your own people polls.

First, choose a topic that interests your family. Then, designate a pollster and help him or her decide on some relevant questions.

For more fun, pollsters might use an empty paper towel tube for a "microphone." Or, if you own a tape recorder or a video camcorder, you might actually record the interviews and play them back later.

You might focus on serious issues, such as current events, or fanciful ones, such as your favorite prehistoric animals. You can alternate between giving your actual opinions and making up zany responses. Your opinions might not change the world—but at least you can be a part of the democratic process.

Radio Days

229 People Prizewinners

Subject: History
Preparation: Make a ballot box

You don't have to be a history buff to appreciate legendary great figures. Your family can hold an election at the dinner table to determine their own "People Prizewinners."

Have your family nominate candidates for the following titles: Greatest Past President, Best Leader, Most Advanced Thinker for His or Her Time, Outstanding Inventor, Person Who Most Changed History, History's Most Unsung Hero, and Historical Figure You Wish You'd Met. To jump-start the process, you can offer the first three or four nominees in each category. This is also a good opportunity to discuss the contributions made by various historical figures.

Family members can write down their choices on pieces of paper and slip them into the ballot box. Then have someone tabulate the scores and announce the winners. Which great people will find new fame at your dinner table tonight?

---

230 Pet People

Subject: Zany Stuff
Preparation: None

Some animals have actually adopted other animals as pets. (Koko the Gorilla had a pet kitten.) How about imagining a little "role reversal?" Here's a neat dinner table question that's bound to generate some wild answers:

Why don't animals keep people as pets?

Subject: Science and Nature
Preparation: An assignment a day or so before

Are your kids interested in pets? Here's an activity that will get them talking and thinking about some unusual additions to your home.

After dinner, ask everyone to pick an unusual pet—something like a rhinoceros, a giant sea turtle, or a gibbon. Then have each person describe what it would be like to care for such an animal. Pet tenders should answer questions like: Why would the animal make a good pet? What would you feed it? Where would it sleep? What would be the difficulties in caring for the animal? What would you do to amuse it and show it affection? How would having this animal around the house change your family's routine?

(Should you not be able to answer some of these questions, encourage the pet tender to do some library research and report back at the next meal.)

Another way to play is to write down various animal's names on slips of paper and place them in a paper bag. Let everyone draw a slip or two and try to explain how he or she would care for the animal.

Now then, how would you groom a Canadian moose?

Show and Tell

Subject: Science and Nature
Preparation: None

Are we the only species with an imagination? Whether or not you have pets at your house, you can ask your family the following question at your dinner table:

What do cats, dogs, fish, parakeets, and other animals think about when they're alone?

Fifty Questions

233 Pioneer Family

Subject: Self and Emotions
Preparation: None

Congratulations! NASA has selected your family (from thousands of qualified applicants) to be the first settlers on a nearby planet! You'll be alone for a while; no other space flights have been scheduled to go there for at least ten years, and you won't be able to return to Earth before then.

Shipwrecked

Your spaceship is small, and you'll have to pack many essentials so there will only be enough room left over for each space traveler to take one personal possession. Which object, of all the things that you own, would you choose to take with you?

Now ten years have gone by. An Earth spaceship is coming, but it's big enough to carry only one person (who can stay for only a week). Who would your family most want to see? What would you want that person to bring with him or her?

Someday we're sure to be reading about you in our history books!

---

234 Play Time

Subject: Readin', Writin', 'Rithmetic
Preparation: None

Have you ever wanted to try your hand at acting? Well, here's a way to hit the boards without the bother of applying greasepaint, memorizing lines, building a set, or sewing a costume.

After dinner, simply render a dramatic reading of your favorite book or play. When reading the description, you're the narrator. When reading the dialogue, then you become the character who's speaking.

Family members can take turns reading paragraph by paragraph, or each can be assigned to read the lines of a different character. Or, have participants take turns playing the same characters, and notice the differences in each person's rendition.

However you do this activity, you'll find it a great way for your family to "try on" characters of different ages, nationalities, and personalities, and challenge their acting abilities to the utmost. Curtain!

Dinner Theater

235 Please Say Thanks

Subject: Ethics
Preparation: None

What are the nicest words in your vocabulary? We nominate two possibilities: "please" and "thank you." Have your family members take turns answering the following question at the dinner table:

Why are the words "please" and "thank you" so important?

Fifty Questions

Plot Swap 236

Subject: Arts and Media
Preparation: None

Have you read any good books lately, or have you seen any neat movies? No one has the time to read everything that's published or to see every new movie, but "plot swapping" can help your family stay abreast of "what's hot and what's not."

Have a family swap meet night, with everybody bringing a different book or movie plot to the table. (You might want to help kids choose the books and movies in advance.) Then, take turns sharing the stories, setting a three-minute time limit for each. Grownups might want to help younger children out by asking questions, such as, "What time did Cinderella's fairy godmother tell her she had to be home by? Who did Cinderella meet at the ball?" etc. Be careful not to reveal a surprise ending without getting permission to do so first—others might want to read the book or see the movie for themselves, after you've made it sound so appealing!

Use what you learn to plan family reading time or family movie days. Now, isn't this better than arguing about who gets the remote control?

Soapbox

237 The Plot Thickens

Subject: Story Making
Preparation: None

Family Book Works

How would you like to collaborate on a story with literary figures like E.B. White, Beverly Cleary, and Mark Twain?

Just pick your favorite author, open one of his or her books, and have someone read aloud the first paragraph or two. Or they can simply set up the story by paraphrasing the introduction. For instance, "An old woodcarver carved a block of wood one day to make a puppet, and he named his creation Pinocchio."

Have the family continue the story from that point in their own words. You can stick to the original plot, with participants taking turns telling the story. Or, you can change the plot entirely. In your version of the story, Pinocchio might be a Harvard professor who wins the Nobel Peace Prize on his fiftieth birthday. You might also add new characters and a surprise ending to your story.

Just imagine the plots you can weave with characters like Stuart Little, Beatrice and Ramona, or Tom Sawyer.

---

238 Pop Goes the Quiz

Subject: Current Events
Preparation: None

Gazette Games

You've already read the paper, so you know just about everything there is to know about the day's news—or do you? Here's how you can find out what you might have missed.

After dinner, divide the newspaper into sections, with everyone taking several pages. Then, have each person search his or her section for a bit of information that everyone else might have missed. When everyone has come up with one or two news items, take turns quizzing each other. Was there an important development in the sports world? An unusual local event in the making?

Another way to do this activity is to have everyone write his or her question down for a family quiz. How does your family score on the "dinnertime details" exam?

Subject: Readin', Writin', 'Rithmetic
Preparation: None

Why wait until your next family vacation to send postcards to your relatives and friends? Some night over dinner, take a few minutes to say, "Having a good time, and wish you were here."

You can start off with blank postcards from your local post office, or you can make your own by recycling cardboard boxes or the backs of old greeting cards. Draw a vertical line down the middle of your postcard.

To the left of the line, write a message that everyone agrees on, or have each family member contribute a line. The name and address of the person who's receiving the postcard go to the right of the line, along with a postage stamp. Turn the postcard over, have someone draw a picture that illustrates the message or just looks nice, and it's ready to be sent.

You don't have to have much to say—just letting your family and friends know that you're thinking about them is saying enough.

Family Communications

Subject: Politics
Preparation: None

If some country is having serious problems, should the United States get involved? Here are some ideas for starting a table talk debate over the matter:

It's Not Our Problem

Another country's problems are just that—its own problems—and the people of the United States should stay out of them. We probably don't understand all of the issues and couldn't be of much help anyway. We also have enough troubles of our own to solve.

It's One World

We all live in one world and share the same planet—any serious problems in one country affect us all. If we see leaders misusing their power and people being mistreated, then the United States needs to get involved to try to solve the problem.

Great Debates

242 Presidential Honor

Subject: Politics
Preparation: None

Great Debates

Should the president of the United States always tell the public everything, or are there times when our highest elected official should withhold the truth for our own good?

The President Is Obligated to Tell the Truth

The people of the United States elect the president to be truthful at all times. If some important decision is being made that affects us all, the president should call a news conference and tell us about it. The president should answer any questions people may ask fully and truthfully—that's a basic responsibility.

The President Should Protect Us First

The people elect the president to preserve and protect the country above all else. If some important decision is being made that affects us, and our knowing about it could cause panic, the president should simply do what needs to be done, and tell us about the decision later.

---

241 Pre-Birthday Thoughts

Subject: Just for Fun
Preparation: None

Fifty Questions

Do your family members enjoy fathoming the unfathomable? Here's a sure thought-stretcher that will especially tantalize the younger folks at your dinner table. Ask the question:

Where were you before you were born?

Subject: History
Preparation: None

Is your family up on its knowledge of our nation's presidents? Here's a chance to find out.

During or after dinner, choose a family member to be "it." That person should bring to mind a specific president. If younger children are playing, the most famous presidents would be the best choices—Washington and Lincoln. But if there are children in the midst of their American history studies, try a lesser known figure.

Next, go around the table taking turns asking questions aimed at revealing the president's identity. Was he in charge during a war? Was he considered successful? What was he most known for?

So, who's the famous president who played with lightning and wrote that almanac? None, that we know of—unless Benjamin Franklin was elected president secretly!

Guessing Games

Subject: Family Circle
Preparation: None

If a good friend tells you about a serious problem and then makes you promise to keep it a secret, should you respect the request or try to get your friend some help? Here are some ideas for starting a table talk debate over the matter:

Secrets are Sacred

If you are sworn to secrecy by a friend, you shouldn't tell anyone under any circumstances. If you do tell someone, that friend and others will never trust you to keep a secret again. And if the friend needs some help, you could always convince him or her to tell someone else—like a parent, teacher, or guidance counselor.

Get This Kid Some Help

Even if you are sworn to secrecy, if your friend is in real trouble and needs some help, you should tell someone. You could probably think of a way that your friend's parents or a teacher could approach him or her without mentioning your name. You owe it to your friend to do so.

Great Debates

Subject: Money Matters
Preparation: None

Great Debates

A lot of people think they have to earn a lot of money in order to be happy. Some people choose their jobs on the basis of how much money it pays. Other people say that money isn't everything and that other things are more important, like whether or not what you do makes you happy. Find out what the "green" means to people in your family.

The Root of ALL Evil

Money is bad. If there were no such thing as money, then there would be no wars and no hunger. People would get along with each other and treat each other as equals. Things would be better under the barter system.

For the Greater Good

Money isn't the reason for evil—there was sickness and hunger long before currency was invented. Money can be used for good—to cure diseases, to build houses and roads, to educate people, and to create jobs. It's not money that's the root of all evil, it's the misuse of money.

Subject: Self and Emotions
Preparation: None

Wise words to ponder:

Do not forget little kindnesses, and do not remember small faults.

Great Thoughts

Start a great dinner table discussion by asking:

1. Have you ever forgotten about all the nice things a person had done when you got angry at him or her?

2. How does it feel to get mad at people you love?

3. After you've had a silly argument with a friend or family member, how can you remind yourself of the things you really like about that person?

Subject: Arts and Media
Preparation: None

Radio talk shows are more popular than ever. Why not get in on the trend?

Choose a likely talk show host from among your ranks—the rest of the family can become the announcer/sidekick or guests. The host can interview guests one-on-one about their lives, their occupations (real or imagined), or the reasons for their "fame" or "fortune." Alternatively, he or she can moderate a lively discussion among all of the family members about a topical issue.

You can create titles for each segment, such as "She Built a Pyramid out of Wooden Blocks." And don't forget to include a "controversial" segment or two, such as "Parents Who Help with Homework."

Remember to have everyone take turns at being the host, sidekick, and guests. Then, sit back and enjoy the show!

Radio Days

Subject: Science and Nature
Preparation: None

Are we spending too much time and money on the space program? Some people say that we're reaching for the stars and forgetting about the earth. What does your family think about this intergalactic debate?

Forget Space
We can't afford to explore outer space. Until everyone on Earth has enough to eat and a clean, safe place to live, we should forget about space programs and the like.

Explore Space
Astronauts are today's pioneers, and space travel is a great adventure. Through our space program we're making scientific breakthroughs that will improve our life on this planet. We can't stop exploring—there's too much to be gained.

Great Debates

Subject: Readin', Writin', 'Rithmetic

Preparation: Make a ballot box

Cast Your Vote

What's the best article or section in your local gazette? Inquiring minds want to know.

Have your family nominate their choices for: Most Entertaining Newspaper Section, Story of the Day, Most Useful Fact in Today's Paper, Horoscope Most Likely to Come True, Funniest Cartoon or Article, and Best Advice in Today's Column. If your family typically reads more than one newspaper, then you might want to add a Best Newspaper category.

Have voters write down the categories and their choices, then put the slips of paper inside the dinner table ballot box. Then, sort them by categories, tabulate the votes, and announce the winners.

If anyone missed reading the latest editions of family favorites, then make it policy to "route" all future issues to each family member's attention!

Subject: Books and Literature

Preparation: None

Reading a book is just like watching it on TV or in the movies—or is it? Some people think so. Others say that TV and movies never do justice to books and that reading is far more important anyway. What's your read on this issue?

A Story's a Story

Television and movies are more fun than books. We can see fairy tales, plays, and books come to life on the screen. It's the same story. Why not take advantage of the special effects that television and movies have to offer?

Books Are Better

People should spend more of their time on books, because we learn more by reading than we do from television and movies. Reading teaches us to use our imaginations, to think for ourselves, and to express things clearly. Also, if we only watched television and movies, people would miss out on stories that have been with us for generations.

Great Debates

Subject: Books and Literature
Preparation: None

Your children are bound to be reading—both for school and for fun. This is a chance for them to challenge each other on your knowledge of great—or just fun—literature.

During dinner, choose a family member to be "it." That person thinks of one of his or her favorite book titles and gives a series of clues about it, while the others take turns guessing the book's identity. (Older children might choose something a bit obscure, like a textbook from school that his or her siblings might have used earlier, while younger children might opt for a recent bedtime story.)

Alternatively, you might offer clues about an author (What nineteenth-century woman wrote a semi-autobiographical novel about four young sisters growing up during the Civil War? Louisa May Alcott) or a fictional character (What famous spider befriended a pig named Wilbur? Charlotte). See how well your family can read not only books but also each other!

Guessing Games

Subject: Family Circle
Preparation: Look in a book

Are there some real characters in your family, or interesting relatives that your children have never had the opportunity to meet in person? Well, here's a way to "bring" these people to the dinner table.

After "assigning" topics the day before—say, a great-aunt, second cousin, or someone else who has made an impression—and giving your family time to "research" the subjects, it's time to share the results around the table. Take turns explaining what makes "your" relative special. Perhaps you can find a photo (or draw a picture). Does the person look like anyone else in the family? Does his or her personality remind you of anybody at the dinner table?

Perhaps you can plan a phone call to a relative to learn more about him or her. Wouldn't a long-lost cousin appreciate hearing from you and receiving an update on family news?

Show and Tell

253 Repeat the Rhythm

Subject: Singalong

Preparation: None

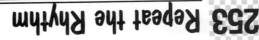

Game Time

Here's a musical game that is guaranteed to liven up your dinner table. Try it the next time you have guests—they may have some fun songs to share!

After dinner, choose someone to start off the game by clapping out a rhythm. The next person copies the rhythm exactly, clapping out the same beat, then changes the rhythm a bit and "gives" it to the next person. That person "takes" the new rhythm, copies it exactly, then changes it a bit and "gives" it to the next person. Go around the table, ending with the person who started. How does the final rhythm compare with the rhythm you started with? Can anyone remember and clap the original rhythm correctly?

After you get this game going with simple beats or songs, and everyone gets the hang of it, add some more complicated rhythms. Who knows—you might have a future percussionist in your family!

---

254 Responsible Television?

Subject: Current Events

Preparation: None

Should television networks and producers be required to create more educational programming? Here are some ideas for starting a table talk debate over the matter:

Great Debates

Television Junk is OK

Everyone knows that much of what is on television is entertainment-oriented, and is not designed to be educational. If producers are forced to create educational programming, then television will probably be pretty boring. Kids get enough of that at school. Plus, there's plenty of educational stuff on TV already.

Television Should Be Better

Everyone knows that kids watch too much television and that it is not only silly, but sometimes it's violent and unhealthy. There is no reason why programs couldn't be both entertaining and educational. Television should be used to help us learn and expand our thinking, not just wow and dazzle us.

255 Right to Vote

Subject: Politics
Preparation: None

The law says young people can't vote until they're eighteen years of age. Should kids be allowed to vote at an earlier age? Have your family debate this question:

No!
Voting is a right that all grownups have—but it's also an important responsibility. Grownups know more, so they can make better choices than kids. If we let kids vote, then kids might make the wrong decisions. We could elect people who couldn't do the job, and then the country would be in trouble.

Great Debates

Yes!
Many kids know more—and care more—than grownups do about issues like the environment, war, and hunger. If kids are old enough to drive a car at age sixteen in some states, they should be allowed to take part in elections, too. Maybe grownups ought to listen to kids for a change about who and what to vote for.

Robin Hood   256

Subject: Ethics
Preparation: None

If stealing is always wrong, then was Robin Hood—the legendary character who stole from the rich and gave to the poor—a bad guy? Here's an interesting question to ponder at the dinner table:

Why do some people take things that don't belong to them—and is it ever okay to do so?

Fifty Questions

Subject: Just for Fun

Preparation: None

Ever wonder what it was like back in prehistoric times? Well, maybe you can't step into a time machine, but you can sure let your imagination fly with this dinner table activity.

After dinner, have all of your family members pretend that they're part of an archaeological team that has just discovered a remarkable fossil. The fossil proves to be millions of years old. What's so remarkable about this find is that instead of finding bones or insects imprinted in the rock, you find . . . tire tracks. How could this be?

Have each member offer a hypothesis—maybe an extraterrestrial came to visit? Or perhaps dinosaurs possessed a super-intelligence we never knew about? Then have everyone take a vote on the theories, in the following categories: Most Imaginative, Most Implausible, Funniest, etc. (Be sure to solicit category ideas from everyone at the table before the vote.) Then submit your ideas to the family "Journal of Preposterous Ideas"—perhaps you'll earn a commendation!

Subject: Just for Fun

Preparation: None

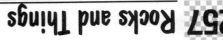

Here's an easy word game you can play while everyone is waiting for a meal to be served up or while the dishes are being cleared.

First, choose someone at the dinner table to pick a category to start off the game. Then, take turns thinking of something in that category—starting with something that begins with "A." For names, the words could be Alice or Alex. Next, try something that begins with "B"—Bob or Barney; then "C"—Carol or Cliff. When you've worked your way all through the alphabet, have someone pick your next category and begin again. "A"—apricots; "B"—broccoli. And so on.

A variation of this activity is to take turns, using a single letter at a time, until no one can think of another thing in that category—before you move on to "B." Prepare yourself; you could be in for a long wait!

Subject: Ethics
Preparation: None

What would it be like to make decisions that affect millions of people? If you want to find out, ask this question at the dinner table:

If you were the president, what are the three most important rules you would make for everyone—kids and grownups—to follow?

Fifty Questions

Subject: Role Play
Preparation: None

If you and your family do much space traveling. . . this could happen to you.

Let's say that you and your family make a surprise landing in a distant galaxy on the planet Salt. You don't speak the language and you're low on provisions. The first thing you discover is that, although the Saltites are friendly, they eat and drink only salty water (they're willing to share). How would you and your family ask them (using only body language) for bread and fresh water? Fruit? Vegetables? Your favorite foods?

Suppose you've been stranded for months now and you're getting pretty bored. How would you let the Saltites know that you're starving for entertainment, and what would you ask them for?

Well, some things might be tough on Salt . . . but at least your food would never be too bland!

Shipwrecked

Subject: School Matters
Preparation: None

We spend so much of our childhoods at school that it makes sense to preserve the memories. And to fudge them a little here and there, if necessary.

Devote a chapter of your Family Album to individual school "transcripts." (Yes, these are on the record—the family record!) Over dinner, have family members take turns "interviewing" each other to find out each person's favorite subjects, most influential or best-loved teacher, and favorite extracurricular activities. Note what schools he or she attended (don't forget to include dates), most memorable year, and so on. Include special achievements, revealing or funny stories, escapades, and the names of any partners-in-crime. You might write something like, "Mom was an excellent history and math scholar, but she's best remembered for starring as Maria in her junior class production of West Side Story—and for forgetting to wear her costume shoes on opening night!"

Subject: School Matters
Preparation: None

What's the Plan?

You may already have a yearly ritual—planned or unplanned—of shopping for the new school year. Getting everyone involved in the budgeting could prove to be educational for the whole family.

During this dinnertime conversation, find out which items everyone will need before school begins again, such as notebooks, pencils, and art supplies. Now choose someone as scribe and pull out the plan book. Begin a list of items you need or hope to get.

For older children, you might also want to include some way to earn money for extra items. One family we know budgets only for discount store products; if anyone wants a pricey brand-name item instead, he or she needs to find a way to pay the difference. That's a good lesson in planning—and in stretching dollars!

Subject: Current Events
Preparation: Pass out newspaper sections

In today's madcap, fast-paced world, maybe the news would make more sense—if it were scrambled!

Before dinner, try giving everyone in the family a section of the newspaper—sports, real estate, advice, business—and have each person cut out a sentence or two. Toss these into a paper bag, shake, empty the bag onto the table, and line up the clippings however they fall.

There's your outline for today's "big story," which should be read during dinner. The story can be serious, funny, or silly—you decide by filling in the blanks. Try coming up with a headline. Reshuffle and start again as many times as you'd like . . . who knows what you'll create!

Gazette Games

Subject: Arts and Media
Preparation: None

If you see it on the six o'clock news, does that make it true? Here are some ideas for starting a table talk debate over the matter:

If You See Something It Must Be True
If something happens and a television crew is on the scene filming the event for the news, then the public is getting the best account possible—next to being there themselves. Sure, there must be some editing—but editors are responsible for assuring that they preserve the event accurately.

Television News Is Often Misrepresentative
Television news is only as accurate as the people who put it together. First, there's the reporter and camera crew—do they "see" it all? Then, there's the reporter and editor—how do they decide to tell the story? Finally, there's the producer and editor—how do they decide to "sell" the story? We should never believe what we see on TV news until we can find out more about it.

Great Debates

Subject: Self and Emotions
Preparation: None

Wise words to ponder:

Seize the day, put no trust in the morrow.

Start a great discussion by asking:

1. Do you think we're more likely to put off things we want to do or things we don't want to do? Why?

2. How about the things we want today but cannot have—is it possible that we could change our minds, or that something else could come to seem better?

3. How about something that's offered today—a trip with a friend, a day spent with a grand-parent—that you have to say no to . . . will the opportunity ever be the same?

Subject: Role Play
Preparation: Clip newspaper articles

Does your family like to ham it up at the dinner table? If so, try playing the roles of characters out of the pages of to-day's newspaper.

Have somebody clip appropriate stories from the paper about famous or interesting people. Read or paraphrase the first article so everyone can hear, then choose some-one to portray the article's lead character. How would he or she sound, move, and think? Have the person talk about his or her life or about the event that led to his or her name appearing in the newspa-per. Was it exciting, scary, heroic, or impressive?

Now each family member can take turns asking the character questions. For example, "How does it feel to be the Queen of Eng-land? What is a typical day at Buckingham Palace like? What's your favorite thing about being Queen? What's your least favorite?" After each participant has found a character, improvise a mini-play. See how it feels to dine with royalty, elected officials, and other movers and shakers. Hope everyone remembers their ta-ble manners!

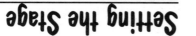

Subject: Just for Fun
Preparation: None

When is a door not a door? When it is a rectangle. See what other shapes everyday objects bring to your young child's mind.

During dinner, have your family take turns choosing a shape to search for around the room or house. For instance, how many things can you find in the kitchen that are squares? Food boxes and picture frames could qualify. How about circles? Dishes, bowls, and jar lids fall into this category. How about triangles? Pie slices, folded napkins, and china patterns may fit this description.

Of course, you can make the activity more interesting for older siblings by adding challenging shapes or by opening up certain other rooms to the search. Or, take out pencils and paper and see who comes up with the most items in a particular shape category.

So, how many ovals do you see—remember to include the face of everyone at the dinner table!

Game Time

Subject: Special Days
Preparation: None

Holidays can often end up making us feel harried, with parties, and baking and shopping. With a plan in hand, this holiday season can include ways to share your family's good fortune with others.

Open up this dinnertime conversation by considering some of the people who you know are less fortunate than yourselves—people who are alone, elderly, or sick. Then discuss how your family could make a difference this holiday season. Can anyone volunteer time once a week? After selecting someone as scribe, list the possibilities in a plan book. These could include a visit a week to a nursing home or helping out at a shelter.

If time is a problem at your house, perhaps your plan could mean assigning everyone to participate in an annual clearing-out of toys, clothes, and household items. The proceeds could be donated to your family's designated cause. Aren't the holidays even more fun with just a little bit of planning—and sharing?

What's the Plan?

Subject: Readin', Writin', 'Rithmetic
Preparation: Clip coupons

Playalong Junk Mail

Here's how you and your family can "shop 'til you drop"—without going downtown, entering a mall, or ever spending a cent.

Just gather some catalogs or coupons. Have a family member choose an item secretly and give a clue about what the object is. For younger children, someone might say, "I've just bought something red." He or she can then add other clues ("you can eat it," or "it grows on trees," or "you can make cider out of it") until somebody figures out what item was bought (in this case, an apple).

Alternatively, you could have your family guess the price of the item you've "bought." You might say, "I've just bought some new shampoo, and I got a real bargain." Have family members take turns guessing the cost, while you say "higher" or "lower." Whoever guesses the real price gets to buy the next mystery item.

How quickly can your family guess which items you've purchased or how much money that you've spent? Well, some families think alike when it comes to shopping!

Subject: Family Circle
Preparation: Make a ballot box

Cast Your Vote

What are your family's favorite ways to share time together? Why not take a vote to find out?

Have your family nominate candidates for the following: Best Family Sharing Time of the Day, Weekly Family Time Most Looked Forward To, Most Outstanding Family Sharing Time Ever, Most Laugh-Producing Way to Spend Family Time Together, Best Family Activity That You'd Like to Enjoy More Often, and All-Weather Favorite Family Sharing Activity. (In case your family is shy about starting the nomination process, you can begin by offering three or four possibilities in each category.)

By secret ballot, have your family cast their votes in each category and put them into the dinner table ballot box. Tabulate the scores and announce the winners.

What have you learned about family sharing that can make your times together even more special?

Subject: Food
Preparation: Clip coupons

Now that you've finished your dinner, how about a little food shopping? It's always better to visit a supermarket when you're not hungry. Actually, with this shopping exercise, you don't even have to leave your chair.

Before dinner, have everyone clip food coupons from the paper or grocery store circulars. Place the coupons in a pile, face down and shuffle them up (you'll need at least five per person). Then draw one of the coupons as you would a card from a

deck, and announce the food. Continue around the table until all of the coupons have been collected. Each person now has the "makings" (perhaps) of a

meal. Allowing a few additions from their pantry or refrigerator, have each person announce the enticing meal he or she plans to make using all the food they just "bought" at the store.

Pretty tricky if you've drawn five coupons for peas. How about split pea soup and salad, followed by pea supreme with creamed peas, and ending up with green pea meringue pie. Yum!

Gazette Games

Subject: Food
Preparation: None

Are there any food pioneers in your family? Then share some of your discoveries with your family. See whether you can improve upon a classic. For instance, the ever-popular PB&J can easily become a peanut butter/jelly/marshmallow/banana/chocolate sandwich, with puffed rice cereal on top to give it that extra crunch. Share some of your own alterations.

Another idea is to assign each family member a course and see how many wacky ideas he or she can come up with for each one. Entree ideas might include such silly recipes as Frozen Pickle Pizza, Pepperoni and Mushroom Cookies (with or without chocolate chips), or Steve's Leafy Green Radish Surprise. See what else you can add to the zany menu.

Your recipes will certainly add new zest to your family's meal planning.

Game Time

Subject: Zany Stuff
Preparation: None

Remember "Pig Latin," or some other coded language of your childhood? Here's your chance to pass this special gift along to your children.

During this dinnertime activity, take turns teaching each other "Pig Latin," or make up a similar language of your own.

In case you've forgotten, Pig Latin works like this: The first letter of each word is dropped and tagged onto the end. Pig becomes "ig-pay"; latin becomes "atin-lay." After explaining it, have everyone practice a bit. Then, attempt a "Pig Latin" conversation. (Of course, you're now using Pig Latin to discuss things without your kids' understanding what you're saying.)

Another way to do this activity is to agree on a single sound substitution, such as "oo" for all vowels in nouns.

Even your child will get the message when you say, "To-night we're having spoogooti with mootbools for soopoor!"

Subject: Singalong
Preparation: None

With today's technology (and some help from your family), everyone in your house can look and sound like a professional vocalist, even if he or she can't sing on key.

Simply have one family member stand or sit off to one side (or hide under the table) and sing a song, while another performer takes center stage and lip-synchs. Choose a song that everyone knows, so that the pretender will be able to move his or her mouth in time to the words and music smoothly and will appear to be actually singing.

Or, if you have a favorite musical tape or recording, you can play it and have family members lip-synch to that instead.

A variation of this is karaoke, where a family member or a tape provides the music for a familiar song, and everyone takes turns singing the words with the accompaniment. You can practice some neat moves, too, like the "Moonwalk" or whatever else might go with the songs.

See how easy it is for your family to make beautiful music together—without making a sound!

Dinner Theater

275 Siskel and You

Subject: Arts and Media
Preparation: None

Do you ever pick a movie based on a reviewer's comments? Here's your chance to play the critic and make your own observations and recommendations.

Clip a newspaper review about an appropriate film. After dinner, read the review aloud. If your family has seen the movie, do you agree with the newspaper's critique? What would you add to it? If you haven't seen the movie, would you want to on the basis of the review? Why or why not?

Next, have everyone pitch in and review something else that the family saw recently. Or, let each family member try his or her hand at writing a short review (this is an especially good idea if everyone has strong and differing opinions).

Two thumbs up for initiative!

Gazette Games

Snowed In 276

Subject: Just for Fun
Preparation: None

Imagine that a huge blizzard struck, causing school and work to be called off for the whole winter. You and your family can't leave the house until the spring thaw arrives (months from now), and no one can come visit. But the pantry's loaded with plenty of food and you have everything you could possibly need right at home.

Have everyone take turns telling how the family would spend the winter days. (Since no one has any outside responsibilities, everything you do is strictly for fun.) If you plan to spend a lot of time talking, what subjects would come up? What kinds of arts and crafts would you make? What games would you play? How would you spend your private time?

Would there be any disadvantages to spending the winter snowed in? Are there any things or people in the "outside world" that you would especially miss? How would your family keep from getting "cabin fever?" What would be the first thing you'd do when you could leave the house?

Enjoy your wintry "vacation!"

Shipwrecked

Subject: Just for Fun

Preparation: None

Have you ever been caught off guard by a snowstorm? It's no fun to trudge home from school or work in the snow when you haven't worn boots—but you can certainly enjoy the snow if you're prepared for it.

Before the snow falls, hold a family dinnertime planning session. Select someone as scribe and pull out the plan book to make a list of snow-related activities before the snow melts next spring. Perhaps there are some sledders and skiers in your house. Are there sledding hills nearby? A toboggan run? Maybe this is the year to sign up for ski lessons or take a weekend trip. A winter visit to your favorite summertime park could make an interesting outing—you could even reserve a shelter, build a fire, and have a winter picnic!

As part of your plan, you might assign everyone to keep a look-out for winter festivals and celebrations that include snow and ice. Who knows, perhaps there is an ice sculptor in your midst!

Subject: Singalong

Preparation: None

In this singalong game, your family's musical vocabulary will be put to the test. You might be surprised at the number of songs everyone knows!

The object is to think of a number of songs containing a specific word. Here's how it works: Take turns around the table selecting a word (or category), such as blue or colors; Chicago or cities; Louise or girls' names. Then take turns trying to think of a song that contains the word or category. Like—"Blue Moon," "Blue Suede Shoes," and so on.

Of course, the simplest way to play this game is just to take turns thinking of the song titles, but this activity works best if you can also sing (and, if necessary, teach family members) the song.

Game Time

279 Sorry!

Subject: Ethics
Preparation: None

Although everyone sometimes make mistakes, it takes a big person to say, "I'm sorry." Have your family ponder this at the dinner table:

Why is it so important to apologize if you've done something wrong, or if you've hurt someone's feelings?

Fifty Questions

Space Explorers 280

Subject: Science and Nature
Preparation: None

During this dinner table time travel, imagine that you have been sent to the early eighteenth century to reveal to great minds like Ben Franklin that people would one day travel to the moon, where they would walk around and take soil samples and even plant a flag.

Be sure to mention to Ben (played by one of the parents) that the first moonwalk took place in 1969 after many years of sending satellites into orbit. Explain that there is no air in space, but that spacecraft contain their own air supply. You might mention gravity. And of course, he'll want to hear all about how the moon is really just a barren rock with lots of craters, no life forms that we can recognize, and no green cheese.

Time Travel

Subject: Special Days
Preparation: None

Family Album

Wouldn't it be great if every day were a holiday? Well, at your house it can be. Have everyone at the dinner table agree on one or more events that should be celebrated—say, something that a family member accomplished or experienced during the day. For example, you might declare "Planting the Garden Day," "Sam's Maiden Voyage Down the Hill on His Bike Day," or "Wendy's Excellent History Class Presentation Day." Discuss ways that the whole family can observe and honor the event, then have a "scribe" write them up in the Family Album.

Perhaps a special badge could be made after dinner with a ceremonial pinning, or the scribe might enter the event into a special "holiday calendar." An impromptu song or speech might also be in order, as would a certificate designed by the younger members of the household.

How about this one: "George Cleaned Up His Room Without Being Asked Day!"

Subject: Readin', Writin', 'Rithmetic
Preparation: A dictionary on hand

Play School

Do you have any spelling wizards in the family? Or perhaps some "spell-check enthusiasts" who might appreciate the opportunity to rediscover the dictionary?

During dinner, take turns at the table thinking up interesting themes to learn more about—weather, animals, geology—and pick one for your spelling bee. Come up with a list of words related to the topic and pick a teacher/moderator to conduct the bee. He or she should start with simpler words for the younger contestants, and gradually increase the difficulty for older players. Does your family know the correct spelling of the word, as well as what it means?

For variation, the teacher/moderator can use a favorite book as a spring-board—about dinosaurs or fish, for example—to come up with his or her spell-stumping word choices. Then take turns. You might not learn to spell all the words, but you'll all learn a bit about everyone's favorite subject.

283 Spending Spree

Subject: Money Matters
Preparation: None

How about teaching a lesson in frugal shopping? This activity is a great way to get started.

Before dinner, bring the newspaper to the table and pass out sections so that everyone has several pages of advertisements. Then, have everyone look through the ads and clip items (with prices) that they want and/or need. During dinner, after everyone has a few items selected, give each family member a pretend $25.00 to spend. What would everyone buy? How far does the $25.00 go? And, most importantly, when their cash gets low, can people draw the line between wanting and needing?

Gazette Games

Sports Huddle 284

Subject: Sports
Preparation: None

Everyone has a favorite sport to watch or to participate in. Here's a chance to find out something more about your family's favorites.

During or after dinner, choose someone to be "it." That person thinks of a sporting activity—such as soccer, swimming, or tennis. Then the others take turns asking questions aimed at identifying the sport. Does it involve a ball? Is it played outside or inside? Do players have to wear a uniform? Is it scored, timed or measured?

One way to make this activity work for younger children is to limit the choices to sports or games you have tried. So, has anyone in your family ever played Australian football?

Guessing Games

Subject: Sports

Preparation: Look in a book

Show and Tell

While it seems we have few heroes these days, sports figures tend to fit the slot with young people. Here's a chance for your kids to tell you why.

After "assigning" topics—a favorite basketball player, football player, baseball player, figure skater, swimmer, or gymnast—a day or so before, tonight after dinner share the results of everyone's research. Take turns going around the table and swapping information about each of these athletes. What was the person's greatest moment? Why should we admire him or her? When did the person start his or her sport? There may even be some pictures around the house to share. Then, open up the dinner table talk to a discussion. Has anyone ever seen this person in action? Where? When?

Another way to do this activity is to limit your choices to athletes in your own community. You may even uncover a future Olympian or a minor-league player on the way up!

Subject: Sports

Preparation: Make a ballot box

Cast Your Vote

If you think the Super Bowl is pretty exciting, then just wait until you hold your own "Sportsacular." You won't need pizza and popcorn to make this a thrill—the fun is built in!

Have your family nominate its picks for the following categories: Most Exciting Spectator Sport, Most Improved Team, Most Valuable Player, Most Valuable Coach, Greatest Local Team, Best Stadium, This Year's Game That's Most Likely to Make the History Books, This Year's Best Play, and Most Interesting Sports News Item of the Year. Cast your votes in a secret ballot, add them up, and declare the winners. Hold a similar election for non-professional teams. If you have any not-quite-ready-for-the-big-league players at your dinner table, then this will be especially rewarding. You'll probably want to add to the above categories some of the following: The Number to Watch This (or Next) Season, Most Spirited Team, and Player Most Likely to Make It to Yankee Stadium Someday (or the Astrodome, RFK Stadium, etc.).

Impartiality's not required—just a little home team loyalty!

Subject: Geography
Preparation: None

Recent studies have revealed that our nation's schoolchildren do not know much about where countries are on the globe, much less where the states are on the map. Here's a fun way to enhance your kids' geographical knowledge.

During or after dinner, choose a family member to be "it." (Make sure you give everyone at the table a chance.) It is up to that person to think of one of the states—a place he or she is familiar with—and recall enough information to answer some questions. Maybe it's your favorite vacation state, a place you've heard a lot about on the news lately, or maybe relatives live there.

Next, everyone at the table takes turns asking questions to reveal the state's identity. Is it nearby? Have you been there lately? Is it famous for growing wheat? Is it by an ocean? A lake? Do you know someone who lives there—or perhaps, after this, someone who wants to move there?

Guessing Games

Subject: Geography
Preparation: None

Summertime brings brighter evenings and at least an illusion of more free time. With a little planning, your family can make the most of it!

During this dinnertime conversation, discuss the kinds of activities that make summertime fun. Perhaps there is a beach or lake you've always wanted to visit, a favorite park you wish you went to more often, or an historic site you've always wanted to visit. Then select someone as scribe and pull out the plan book. Go around the table listing ideas for family outings. Next, make a rough schedule, trying to fit them all in. (In order for this one to work well, make sure to include everyone's top choices.)

So, will you finally get to see the famous landmarks you've driven by every day, but have never had a chance to explore? Now's the time!

What's the Plan?

Subject: Ethics
Preparation: None

Twilight Zone

You've all heard the expression about being a "fly on the wall." This activity gives it a new twist.

Imagine that you could hear any conversation you wanted to without being noticed. Have your family discuss the following: Where would you go, and why? Would you feel guilty about eavesdropping? If so, would you do it anyway? Why or why not?

Finally, do you think there might be disadvantages to being a fly on the wall—like hearing things you wished you hadn't such as a surprise for your birthday? Now, if you could choose between having "super ears" and regular ones, which would you choose?

Subject: Neighborhood Awareness
Preparation: None

Take a Letter

Is there a problem in your neighborhood that you believe could be solved rather easily? Here's an activity that will demonstrate the heart of our political process. During dinner, hold a family meeting. Is there an intersection that is always hazardous, or is your community the only one you know of that has no recycling program? Poll your family to identify an appropriate problem. After choosing your cause, pick someone to act as scribe and compose a family letter to the mayor or town councilor. Make certain the letter concisely explains both the problem and the solution in detail—excellent writing practice!

To take this activity a step further, if your family members have an issue they feel very strongly about, write a number of letters (depending on the issue) to your state senator or governor. This might be the perfect opportunity to identify just who these folks are and what they can do for your family. Who knows—this could reach all the way to Washington!

291 Stress Busters

Subject: Self and Emotions
Preparation: None

The sooner we all learn to relax and enjoy ourselves more fully, the better! So now, while your family is lounging around the dinner table, have them discuss the following question:

If someone you know were upset or worried about work or school, what would you tell him or her to do?

Fifty Questions

Subject: Just for Fun
Preparation: None

Here's your chance to create your own family code—great for budding cryptographers.

During or after dinner, take out some paper and pencils and go around the table, soliciting suggestions for a secret coded language. Silverware items or dishes, for instance, could stand in for words, letters, or entire sentences. Say that a fork stands for "help," a spoon for "trouble" and knife for "today." You could create a coded message that read, "Fork," I'm in "Spoon," and need you "Knife." Have your scribe record the codes for posterity.

Another way to do this activity (which will probably appeal to older kids) is for each of you to create your own codes and write messages to each other—making them as tricky as you wish. Then, see whether you can decode them.

Ok, try this one: shoestring, chopstick, two taps on the table. (Now do you know where the chocolate chip cookies are?)

Game Time

Subject: Ethics

Preparation: None

Great Debates

Should journalists be allowed to report the details of famous people's personal lives, or should they be required to keep certain things quiet? Here are some ideas for starting a table talk debate over the matter:

Free Speech, Free Reporting

Anyone who is famous should realize that his or her life is now in the public eye. If the person is looking for fame and fortune, close personal scrutiny is part of the deal. Journalists are just doing their jobs when they tell us about famous people's lives.

Leave People Alone

Just because someone is famous for one thing—like singing or acting—doesn't mean that his or her entire personal life should be open to journalists. Journalists should protect people's privacy and leave them alone, covering only those events that are public.

Subject: Readin', Writin', Rithmetic

Preparation: None

Game Time

Here's a word game that is perfect for new readers and older children alike—you can make it as easy or difficult as your family desires.

During dinner, decide what your game of hangman will include—such as things found at the dinner table (forks, spoons, or salad) or things found in the garden (grass, trees, and the like). Then choose someone to start off the game. That person picks a word from the category you all agreed upon, and the others go around the table and take turns trying to guess what the word is—by guessing one letter at a time. Whoever spells out and solves the word becomes the next person to pick a word for everyone else to guess.

Another way to do this game, of course, is to make your categories as complicated as your family is up for—say, things found under a car's hood, or things in a gymnasium. So who will be the first to figure out the word "dinner"?

Subject: Story Making
Preparation: Clip newspaper photos

Here's how you can prove the old Chinese adage that a picture is worth a thousand words.

First, have someone clip pictures from the newspaper. Be sure to include a variety of photographs and illustrations—people, objects, buildings, maps, and so on. You'll need at least one picture per family member. Place all of the photos into a paper bag, then pass the bag around the table during dinner. Each person chooses one or more pictures.

Begin when somebody has the opening of a story about his or her picture. For example, someone holding a weather map might begin: "It was a glorious summer day and the sun was shining in Montana . . . ." The next person jumps in with a sentence or two about his or her picture ("Three elephants were seen roaming the Montana jungles"), and so on, until everyone has had a turn. Continue until all the pictures have been accounted for.

The next time someone complains that the news is all bad, take out your bag of pictures—your family can instantly fashion all the news that's fit to speak.

Gazette Games

Subject: Health Matters
Preparation: None

Wise words to ponder:

An ounce of prevention is worth a pound of cure.

Start a great dinner table discussion by asking:

1. Against which of life's misfortunes can we take preventive action?

2. Why not just wait till something breaks or we get sick, then fix it or take medicine?

3. If it's easier to prevent certain problems, like illness, than to deal with them once they occur, then why don't we all take the right steps to do so?

Great Thoughts

Subject: Self and Emotions

Preparation: None

W ise words to ponder:

Don't cross the bridge till you come to it.

Start a great dinner table discussion by asking:

1. Can you remember worrying about something that never came to pass?

2. Can you plan for every little detail of everything you do?

3. Is there ever any good reason to worry about what's going to happen next?

Great Thoughts

Subject: Science and Nature

Preparation: None

L ong before people could write, they had language. Knowledge was accumulated by passing it on to one another by word of mouth. Even the great poems attributed to Homer—the Iliad and the Odyssey—were passed on orally well before they were ever written down.

During this dinner table travel, imagine that you have been sent to Ancient Greece to travel with a bard—someone whose job it is to memorize chants, stories, and news to carry from town to town. Your task is to break the news to your companion that the job of bard will cease to exist in the future—it will be replaced by the postal system, telephones, radio, and television. Care to try to convince your friend about the invention of the video phone?

Time Travel

Subject: Just for Fun
Preparation: None

Here's a way to turn fun family secrets into material for your own version of a morning tabloid. Don't have any secrets? No problem. Make something up!

During dinner, take turns around the table whispering a secret to the person next to you. It doesn't have to be anything big—just something that happened or something you did that no one else knows about—yet. Then, after all secrets are told, take turns again around the table, telling the stories aloud—only this time you tell someone else's secret, not your own. Remember, the point here is to have some fun. So, don't hold back: elaborate, colorize, dramatize the events! Then it's up to everyone else to figure out what part of the story is true.

Another way to do this activity is to turn the stories into your own family book of tall tales. Haul out the recycled household paper and have everyone pitch in with some designs and illustrations. Isn't it easy to turn news into fiction?

Game Time

Subject: Just for Fun
Preparation: None

In this high-tech era, it's almost unimaginable that at one time people used the Morse Code to communicate long-distance. Try the code yourselves to send and receive a few important messages across the dinner table. Just tap your silverware together using the following system (dots represent soft taps, dashes represent louder taps). It might be low-tech, but it works!

A •–	M ––	Y –•––
B –•••	N –•	Z ––••
C –•–•	O –––	1 •––––
D –••	P •––•	2 ••–––
E •	Q ––•–	3 •••––
F ••–•	R •–•	4 ••••–
G ––•	S •••	5 •••••
H ••••	T –	6 –••••
I ••	U ••–	7 ––•••
J •–––	V •••–	8 –––••
K –•–	W •––	9 ––––•
L •–••	X –••–	0 –––––

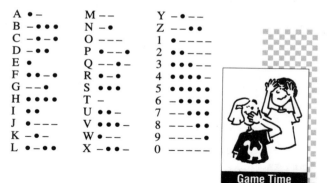
Game Time

Subject: School Matters
Preparation: None

Great Thoughts

Wise words to ponder:

Teachers open the door, but you must enter by yourself.

Start a great dinner table discussion by asking:

1. Have you had a teacher who inspired you to learn additional things about a subject on your own? How did he or she get you to do that? And were others inspired, too, to do extra work?
2. How can teachers make learning exciting, so that kids will want to learn more on their own?
3. Does learning ever stop?

Subject: Friendship
Preparation: None

Great Thoughts

Wise words to ponder:

Three men helping one another will do as much as six men singly.

Start a great dinner table discussion by asking:

1. Can you list two or three chores you do at home that go quickly when you help each other?
2. Can you think of anything that is better done alone?
3. Nowadays people do much more on their own. Why?
4. Wouldn't the world be a better place if people helped each other more? Why is it so hard to do?

303 Telephone Chain

Subject: Just for Fun
Preparation: None

This activity is a classic—but it still provides great fun in our dining room!

During this dinner table game, take turns making up a message. Something like: "Did you hear what happened to our neighbor? He was trying to fix his car, and when he opened the hood, he found three baby squirrels curled up next to the battery." Then, go around the table, each person whispering the secret message to the next. Finally, have the last person in the chain repeat the message out loud. How close did it come to the original?

Another variation on this activity is to pass along tongue twisters (see #319 for suggestions). It will be great fun to see what the last person says when the message starts as nonsense.

Game Time

That May Live in Infamy 304

Subject: History
Preparation: None

Imagine what a news broadcast might have sounded like the day that fire was invented . . . construction was completed on the first Pyramid . . . or a chicken laid the world's first egg.

Your family can create a news broadcast (serious, humorous, or both) detailing an event that occurred long before radio was invented, or one that happened in the more recent past. You can use the announcement of the discovery of fire to describe how cooking kills germs. And you might also get the reaction of local cave people to the prospect of eating cooked meat ("It'll be okay once someone invents ketchup.").

One variation is to make up new endings to real historical events; it would be interesting to learn, for instance, that the first lunar mission in 1969 *did* discover a new life form.

So, if you always believed that there's more to history than what we read, get your reliable news anchors together, turn on the microphones . . . and roll tape!

Radio Days

305 There Are No Bad Foods

Great Debates

Some experts recommend strict diets for everyone—limiting fats and sweets and adding more grains and vege- tables to our diets. But eating junk food is part of being a kid—or is it? Here are some ideas for starting a table talk debate over the matter.

Leave My Junk Food Alone

There are no bad foods—just foods that you shouldn't eat too much of. If you took away hot dogs, chips, fries, burgers, sodas, and candy—what would be left for kids to eat? You'll have plenty of time to eat vegetables and whole wheat bread when you're a grownup.

You Are What You Eat

Whatever you put in your body affects how you feel and grow. It is even more important to eat good foods—whole wheat, fruit, vegetables—when you're young, because that's when you are growing the most. Junk food is just that—junk.

---

306 Things Well Done

Wise words to ponder:

The reward of a thing well done is to have done it.

Great Thoughts

Start a great dinner table discussion by asking:

1. What are some things that you do for yourself— and receive no recognition for? (For example, exercising, hobbies, keeping a journal.)

2. Why do you do certain things just for their own sake?

3. Have you ever been upset at not getting the recognition you felt you deserved?

4. How would the world be a different place if everyone strived to do and be better—just for themselves?

307 Think Summer

Subject: Science and Nature
Preparation: None

Chances are, next spring when you're ready to plant again, all the lessons learned from this year's garden will be about as fresh as canned peas. Use this dinner table discussion as an opportunity to think back about what knowledge you gained, and make a written plan for your next garden. Ask:

Which plants needed more space or less space? Were the squash plants too close to the cukes? Did the tomatoes get enough sun? Should you plant earlier or later? Harvest earlier or later? Which varieties did best? Any varieties that a friend or neighbor successfully planted and harvested? And perhaps most important, "Which plants did the bugs like the best?!"

What's the Plan?

This Is A . . . 308

Subject: Zany Stuff
Preparation: Collect household items

Some say that orators are born, not made. But we believe that with practice, anybody can learn to speak persuasively about almost anything. Here's how to prove it.

First, designate a family spokesperson and have him or her leave the room for two minutes. The rest of the family looks for several objects that can be combined to create a new "invention." A string might be tied to a ruler, or a few spare buttons might be taped to a spatula.

The spokesperson is called back and given three minutes to study the new invention. He or she must then become a salesperson who creates a "strategy" for selling the "whatchamacallit" to the rest of the family, or an inventor who presents the "breakthrough" to the scientific community, the media, or a mass audience at the world's fair. He or she might want to describe all the wonderful things the invention can be used for, how it can improve the public's lives, how much it costs, and how it was made. "Yes, this cotton ball/popsicle stick nose buffer is sure to put a shine on *any* nose!"

Soapbox

Subject: Self and Emotions

Preparation: None

It's easy to judge others' strengths and weaknesses, but it can be difficult to be objective about ourselves. Try this activity for an interesting challenge.

Tell your family about yourself as though they were "meeting you" for the first time. Include the basics, as well as your interests, hobbies, and anything else that you think others would want to know. For a real challenge, reveal the three things you like best about yourself and three things you would most like to change. Have each person at the dinner table repeat the exercise for him- or herself.

When everyone is done, go around the table again. This time have everyone introduce him- or herself *ten years into the future!*

So, what are your kids like a decade from now?

Subject: Readin', Writin', 'Rithmetic

Preparation: None

What's new in your family? Let the world know through a do-it-your-self PR campaign.

Over dinner, compose a press release that focuses on a family announcement, such as the fact that Mom just got a promotion at work or that the family is headed for a weekend at the beach. (Use a tape recorder if you want.) Remember, you're writing this press release to pump up the family's image and impress—so hype the news as much as you'd like.

The press release should have all the elements of a newspaper story, including a snappy headline, and it should answer the questions "who," "what," "when," "where," and "why." Scan a newspaper story to get a feel for the style. At the top of the press release you can use the standard PR phrase FOR IMMEDIATE RELEASE to grab your readers' attention. Make sure that everyone you know gets a copy of your press release. Your family members will certainly find themselves famous among friends and relatives—if not the subject of a features article in your community's newspaper!

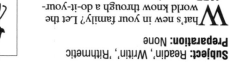

Family Communications

Soapbox

311 This Really Happened

Subject: Self and Emotions
Preparation: None

Storytelling allows us to share poignant moments—and entertain each other in the process.

Have people seated around the table practice the craft of storytelling, taking turns telling about: The happiest day of their lives; the funniest thing that ever happened to them; the scariest thing they've ever seen, done, dreamt, or heard about; the most embarrassing thing that's ever happened to them; or the most exciting thing that's ever happened to them.

A variation is to have one person begin a story, leaving out the ending. Then, everybody else takes turns guessing the outcome. When each person has had a turn at figuring out the ending, the storyteller reveals the actual conclusion.

Your family members can learn a lot about each other by listening and swapping tales. The stories you share now are the family legends and folklore of tomorrow!

Soapbox

Three Wishes 312

Subject: Zany stuff
Preparation: None

Remember the old story about the magic lamp with the genie inside who can grant you three wishes? While you're looking for that lamp, it never hurts to dream aloud.

Have each participant share three heartfelt wishes with the rest of the family. The dreams might be relatively modest (I wish we could have oatmeal cookies for dessert tomorrow, or I wish somebody would help me shovel the driveway), or far-fetched (I wish my bedroom would get clean all by itself, or I wish I were ten feet tall).

Then, have each person tell what would happen if his or her wish were granted. "If we had thirty inches of snowfall, then we'd get three weeks off from school and we'd . . ." Family members can join in the fun by sharing their own ideas and helping to carry each other's fantasies to extremes.

According to the tale of the genie, anything goes—except wishing for more wishes!

Game Time

Subject: Readin', Writin', 'Rithmetic
Preparation: None

This is a great word game for all ages. Even toddlers can understand the fun of rhymes—what do you think makes Dr. Seuss such a big hit? (Be forewarned, this *can* get outrageous.)

During or after dinner, choose someone to start off the game. That person chooses a three-letter word, such as PEN or NUT. Go around the table and see how many words you can think of that rhyme — DEN, GLEN, BEN, HEN or HUT, GLUT, CUT, and so on. Then, when you've exhausted the list, take the same word and see how many words you can think of that begin with the same first letter of the word—for PEN, try pancake, pencil, and so on. Next, when you've exhausted the list, take the same word and see how many words you can think of that end with the same last letter.

While this game does not require pencils and paper, you may want to have everyone complete his or her lists in private. Then, compare lists and share the laughs!

Subject: Just for Fun
Preparation: None

Family Album

It's the year 3000, and an archaeological team has just unearthed a time capsule from the late twentieth century with your name on it. The scientists pry it open and find—whatever you'd like.

Over dinner, your family can decide on the contents of a "time capsule" for the Family Album. "Filling" it (in the minds' eyes) with the things that best symbolize your family. (Because you're not limited to what could fit in a more traditional time capsule, the possibilities are endless: the house, the minivan, videotapes of last summer's vacation, the treehouse in the backyard—or even the whole tree.) Have each person "put in" at least one object until everyone agrees that your family is pretty well represented. Participants can offer each other suggestions—perhaps Dad should include the wild print shirt that he's been saving for the future. Don't forget to date your time capsule and post a warning: Not to be opened until . . . (the agreed-upon time). You probably won't be ready to encounter Dad's shirt until then, anyway!

Subject: Readin', Writin', 'Rithmetic
Preparation: None

Now that so many people have calculators, teachers have to decide whether to allow the devices in the classroom. Calculators can help us get the right answers—but are calculators the right way for kids to get the right answers?

Calculators Belong in the Classroom

We should allow kids to use calculators in the classroom. In this age of computers, there are some things that we don't need to do for ourselves. If a machine can add, subtract, multiply, and divide for us, what's the point in learning how to do math?

Do It the Old-Fashioned Way

Calculators shouldn't be used in math class at all. We can't have a calculator with us all the time, so we need to learn how to do math ourselves. If we don't know how to add, subtract, multiply, and divide, we just becomes slaves to another machine. By using calculators in school, even if the teacher allows it, we cheat ourselves.

Great Debates

Subject: Self and Emotions
Preparation: None

Wise words to ponder:

He who has everything is content with nothing.

Start a great dinner table discussion by asking:

1. Can you think of anyone who seems to have everything? What kinds of "things" do they have?

2. Can you think of anyone who seems content? What kinds of "things" do they have?

3. Why do we believe that having "things" will make us feel differently?

4. List some times when you felt the most content. Where were you? What were you doing?

Great Thoughts

Subject: Ethics
Preparation: None

D o you always tell the truth, the whole truth, and nothing but the truth—no matter what? Some people believe that there's a time and place for everything, even a lie. How does your family feel about this issue, honestly?

Great Debates

Your Nose Will Grow

It's wrong to lie, and if you're caught, no one will ever trust you again. The truth can sometimes hurt, but even little lies can lead to bigger lies, and then there's no stopping.

Case-by-Case Basis

Sometimes, it's okay to fib. A little fib, like telling someone that you like his or her new hairstyle when you don't, can protect someone's feelings. As long as nobody gets hurt, it's sometimes okay to tell a lie.

Subject: Self and Emotions
Preparation: None

I s it better for us to enjoy ourselves now or to plan for the future? It's up to you to decide what's more important to you. But whatever you do, don't put off having this discussion until tomorrow!

Great Debates

Living for Tomorrow

We have to think about the future, even if it means postponing what we want sometimes. If we live only for the present, we might be sorry someday. A little bit of planning and frugal living now can mean the difference between a bright future and an unhappy one.

Living in the Now

All that we'll ever have is the present. If we don't enjoy ourselves now, we never will. If we enjoy each day to the fullest, tomorrow will take care of itself. Otherwise, we'll always be planning for a future that never comes.

319 Tongue Twisters

Subject: Zany Stuff
Preparation: None

Remember "She sells sea shells?" How about "How much wood would a woodchuck chuck?" With nothing more than some time and tongue twisters, you can have some of the zaniest dinner table fun ever.

Before or after dinner, open up the table for sharing some tongue twisters and other verses. (Even simple ones, such as those by Dr. Seuss or Mother Goose, can be challenging to recite accurately at a fast clip.) Traditional tongue twisters include, "She sells sea-shells on the sea shore; the shells that she sells are sea-shells, I'm sure. So if she sells sea-shells on the sea shore, I'm sure that the shells are sea-shore shells." Another good one: "Peter Piper picked a peck of pickled peppers; a peck of pickled peppers Peter Piper picked. If Peter Piper picked a peck of pickled peppers, where's the peck of pickled peppers Peter Piper picked?"

Take turns repeating the twisters more and more quickly until everybody gets tangled up over the words. How well can you handle "Seven silly swans swam silently seaward?"

Game Time

Too Much Fun 320

Subject: Self and Emotions
Preparation: None

Wise words to ponder:

Can we ever have too much of a good thing?

Start a great dinner table discussion by asking:

1. Can something good become the opposite if overdone or overused?

2. Name some things that can easily become too much. (For example, how about chocolate?)

3. List some things that can't be overdone. (For example, how about peace or love?)

Great Thoughts

Transparently Fun

Subject: Zany Stuff
Preparation: None

Twilight Zone

What if you and your family were invisible? How would your lives change?

Have your family discuss the following:

How would you let each other know where you were? Would you take the time to get dressed in the morning? If so, what would you wear? Would you comb your hair? What corners might you be tempted to cut if no-body could see you?

How do you think your lives would change if you were invisible? What would you do that you'd never been able to do before? What might you be able to get away with doing that you shouldn't do—and would you do it any-way? How would your friends feel about you? How would your relationship with them change?

Finally, if you and your family were invisible, could you be beautiful anyway? And how would you convince the "beholders?"

To the Dump

Subject: Science and Nature
Preparation: None

Fifty Questions

We're all becoming aware of the need to create less trash. How much does your family know about the fate of your garbage? Find out with this question—it's sure to open an informative discussion at your dinner table:

What happens to our trash after it gets picked up by the garbage truck (or we take it to the dump)?

Subject: Geography
Preparation: None

The idea of traveling the world may be appealing—but difficult for youngsters to imagine. Here's an activity that will get them thinking about how countries are both different and the same.

During or after dinner, select someone to be "it." That person then thinks of a country. The rest of the family's job is to identify the country by taking turns asking questions. Is it surrounded by ocean? Is it in the Northern or Southern Hemisphere? What is the primary language? Do you know anyone who lives there? Do you regularly eat food from there?

A good way to make this activity a bit more difficult—for an older child or someone studying geography at school—is for the guessers to try to outwit the person thinking of a country. If a guesser asks that person something he or she can't answer, it's the guesser's turn to select a country.

Guessing Games

Subject: Self and Emotions
Preparation: None

Everyone loves to get mail. Which letters would your family members treasure? Find out by asking this question at the dinner table:

If you could write a letter to anyone on the planet (past or present) and get a response, who would you write to?

Fifty Questions

Subject: Story Making

Preparation: None

This is a game your family may be play-ing already—without knowing it!

During or after dinner, take turns telling tales—incidents that really happened or ex-aggerations. You might say, "I was so hun-gry at lunchtime today that I ate two peanut butter and jelly sandwiches and three apples for dessert!" Then everyone else has to decide whether the story is true or made up. When everybody's guesses are in, it's time for the storyteller to confirm the story or 'fess up—and then, perhaps, he or she can further embellish the tale and make it as unbelievable as possible!

Subject: Arts and Media

Preparation: None

Great Debates

The average American family spends nearly seven hours a day in front of the TV set. Is watching television the best possible use of time? Let's see how your family rates television.

I Want My TV

Watching television is an okay use of time. TV teaches us about new places, people, and things that we wouldn't get to see otherwise. TV entertains us—and anyway, if we didn't watch TV, we would often have no idea what other people were talking about.

Unplug It

We spend too much time in front of the tube when we should be doing other, more creative things instead. Television watch-ing is a bad habit, and most people would be better off if they read books, exercised, and found new ways to entertain themselves.

327 Up in Smoke

Have your family leave science aside for the moment and just have fun using your imaginations. Now apply yourselves to this dinner table problem (all attempts, are welcome):

Where does fire go when it goes out?

Fifty Questions

Video/Audio Dinner 328

If you have relatives or friends who don't get to see you very often, why don't you "travel" to their houses—without ever leaving yours? Just produce your own tape during dinner, and when they play it back, it will be almost as though you were there.

You'll need a video camcorder or tape recorder and a family who's eager to ham it up. You might find it helpful to plan what you're going to do—what you're going to talk about or in which order you're going to speak—before the tape is rolling. You can also write a letter on paper first (before dinner), and then take turns reading it aloud. When you finish recording, rewind the tape and send it off.

The recipient will certainly appreciate the surprise visit from your family—even if you didn't remember to call first to say that you were coming!

Family Communications

329 Visitor from the Past

I magine that it's the middle of the night. Your doorbell rings. Opening the door, you discover a person from the past, say Medieval times, who has entered into a "time warp." She lets you know that she'd like to spend a month with your family studying the present and its customs, and that only your family is allowed to know she's there.

Have your family discuss the most important things that she should learn about life today. What do you think she'd be most curious to find out about? Most likely to misunderstand? What major differences will she find between the present and her own time? What will you enjoy most about having her stay with your family? And after she gets back home, perhaps she'll send a post-card through the time warp!

330 Wagon for Sale

W ant to clean out the basement or garage with just the click of a pen? How about placing a classified?

Bring the classified pages of the newspaper to the table and read several ads aloud. Then, during dinner, poll the family on the kinds of things you might want to try to sell. Assign a particular item to each person and have everyone try his or her hand at writing a classified. What kind of words make the item sound saleable? Next, have everyone read his or her ad aloud. Does anyone have the knack for good description?

Of course, you may actually want to place one or two of these classifieds created at the dinner table. Maybe one of your budding copywriters has figured out a way to sell some of the odder gifts given with good intentions but unusual taste.

Gazette Games

Twilight Zone

331 The Walls Have Ears

Subject: Just for Fun
Preparation: None

Some people believe that houses have personality and character. How about yours?

During dinner, choose a room—the kitchen, the living room, the attic, perhaps. Then, improvise a short story about events that might have taken place in the room you picked. Perhaps something amusing or memorable occurred when it was built, or when another family lived in your house. When you've all had time to think of tales, take turns sharing them.

Another way to do this activity is to extend your imaginings to the entire block. Is there something unique about your neighborhood? Perhaps it could be the setting for the next family classic!

Soapbox

Waste Not 332

Subject: Ethics
Preparation: None

Wise words to ponder:

Waste not, want not.

Start a great dinner table discussion by asking:

1. Have you ever regretted throwing something away? Why?

2. What kinds of things should people in the family save—in case they might need them later?

3. How would the world be a different place if we all saved and reused whatever we could?

Great Thoughts

333 Way-out Broadcast

Subject: Role Play
Preparation: None

Radio Days

Our scientists say that radio waves don't stop once they've been broadcast—they just keep traveling on through space. So set the dials on your radio and prepare to receive some far-out signals beamed by folks from another planet (played by your family)!

Your broadcast might include information about your planet—its politics, weather, music, leisure activities, business climate, and so on. What kinds of things do you advertise, and what sorts of editorials do you air? You can include interviews with celebrities, such as sports figures, actors, politicians, or average "people on the street."

Remember that your transmission doesn't necessarily have to be in an earth language. It can be in Pluterian or any other language you can blip up. Your broadcast might even be a jumble of signals from more than one planet—or more than one galaxy. If you think that there's never anything new and interesting on the radio, then conjure up a transmission of your own that's simply out of this world!

334 The Way Home

Subject: Science and Nature
Preparation: None

There are some mysteries in this world that even the greatest scientific minds can't answer. (Perhaps they're just not trying hard enough!) How will your family resolve the following dinner table puzzle:

Why is it that people can get easily lost, but migrating birds and animals can find their way home year after year?

Fifty Questions

335 The Way We Were

Subject: Family Circle
Preparation: None

Every family has some history to share and stories to tell. The Family Album is a perfect place to preserve them.

During and after dinner, poll the family for a favorite memory or a piece of family history to share. Choose a scribe (an older child or parent) and start a page of family history in your new Family Album. Are there people or pets no longer alive who hold a place in your family's hearts? Perhaps a neighbor who moved away or a former teacher can be remembered here.

Be sure to include some small story or piece of history from each family member. For parents, this is a perfect time to pass on memories of your own childhood and stories of relatives both known and unfamiliar.

Another way to share this activity is to include visiting relatives. Next time grandparents or other family members come for a dinner visit, get them to contribute to your Family Album by telling their own family history!

Family Album

Weather or Not 336

Subject: Science and Nature
Preparation: Look in a book

Mark Twain once remarked that "Everyone talks about the weather but nobody does anything about it." Even if you can't change it, the weather can be a fascinating dinner table subject for your kids.

After assigning research topics on weather phenomena—storms, thunder, lightning, hail, rainbows, etc.—have each budding meteorologist at the table explain some of the weather you experience in your part of the country. How about special situations, like tornadoes—what should Dorothy have done when the twister whipped through Kansas?

You can expand the activity by having people relate personal experiences about getting caught in storms or make up stories that illustrate strange phenomenon, like getting chased by "ball lightning" during a jaunt across the desert.

If this activity catches on, don't be surprised to someday see your son or daughter on the local 11:00 news cracking jokes and making forecasts!

Show and Tell

337 Weather Report

Subject: Geography

Preparation: None

Game Time

What is your family's knowledge of life in other places? How about starting with something simple—like the weather? (Although it's not necessary, you may want to bring an atlas to the table for this one.)

After dinner, choose someone to describe the weather for someplace—any place at all. For instance, the person may describe the weather as springtime where you live when it's actually winter. Next, that same person goes around the table and asks for weather reports from around the world (again, real or imaginary places). Someone might ask: What's it doing in Australia? Or, what's the weather in living room window?

Now have everyone tell his or her plans for the day based on the "weather conditions" reported at the table. So, what will you do with the summertime snow drifts piling up outside the living room window?

338 Webster's Tales

Subject: Story Making

Preparation: None

Family Book Works

If you have a dictionary nearby, you also have every great story that's ever been told—the words have just been scrambled.

Over dinner, have your family members find the "right" words to weave a great yarn. Each participant chooses one word at random from the dictionary, while someone else writes them down. Then someone begins telling a story, working in one of the selected words. Each family member takes a turn adding a sentence or two to the story, drawing from the word pool. To continue the story, just begin round two, with everybody choosing a new word.

Alternatively, you can write the words on pieces of scrap paper, place them in a bag, and have people draw the pieces of paper—this adds an air of mystery and chance to the activity.

See what the dictionary muse has in store for your family. One thing is for sure—with a dictionary in the house, you'll never be at a loss for words!

Subject: Law and Justice
Preparation: None

Have you ever wondered what it would be like to be in charge of making the laws of the land? Here's a small-scale opportunity. After dinner, choose a scribe and have your family write a new constitution, complete with all the laws and amendments necessary to run the country fairly and productively. (Of course, don't be surprised if your kids lobby for cessation of dessert limits along with other pressing issues.) While you may not end up with a usable list of laws for the nation, your new constitution may become the starting point for a good discussion of what is perceived as fair rules for children.

For a variation on this activity, consider the constitution more as a list of family laws and amendments. Of course, this may mean a bit more democracy than you're prepared for!

Family Senate

Subject: Self and Emotions
Preparation: None

Wise words to ponder:

Beauty is in the eye of the beholder.

Start a great dinner table discussion by asking:

1. Most of us are pretty critical or at least sensitive about how we look. Why?

2. How important are looks? Can you remember what your friends looked like when you first met them? Do they look different to you now?

3. What if you found out something about an attractive person that made them unlikable? Would he or she still be as attractive?

Great Thoughts

Subject: Careers and Occupations

Preparation: None

How many times are your children asked, "What do you want to be when you grow up?" Here's an activity that will reveal some of the careers they are thinking about—without having to ask that dreaded question!

During or after dinner, choose a family member to be "it." That person imagines for him- or herself a career or occupation. It is then up to everyone else to try to guess what the occupation is. Go around the table and take turns asking: Is the job dangerous? Do you wear a uniform? Do you work during the day? The night? Do you save people's lives?

Another way to do this activity is to include fictional occupations—sorcerers and wizards apply within!

Subject: Just for Fun

Preparation: None

How is your sense of hearing? Just so long as you're not too sensitive to decibel levels, this game is sure to sharpen up your listening skills.

During dinner, choose someone to start off the game. While everyone else in the family closes his or her eyes, the starter finds and brings a noisemaking object into the room, such as a pair of spoons, a flour sifter or a couple of lids from cooking pots. Next, everyone takes turns around the table—without opening their eyes—trying to guess what object is making the noise. When the mystery is solved, it's the next person's turn to try and stump the family! (You can take a break to enjoy your meal between rounds, of course.)

Another way to do this activity is to limit the noisemakers to a category of objects—like things from the kitchen, real musical instruments, or items from a particular drawer. (This approach works well with younger ones.)

How much can you learn about objects with your eyes closed? Well, hearing is believing!

Game Time

343 What's That You Say?

Subject: Zany Stuff
Preparation: None

What if, through some strange accident, your family all began to speak a language that nobody else could understand—and you could no longer understand others?

Have your family start a dinner table discussion about the matter and answer the following kinds of questions. If you wanted to teach the language to others, how would you go about it? And how might you go about relearning the language or languages that you used to know? In the meantime, how would you communicate?

Also, how would you convince your friends, relatives, colleagues, and classmates that you weren't just acting silly, and get them to cooperate with you? What would be your biggest frustration, and how might you deal with the sources of them?

Your kids might be surprised to find that how they say something can be just as important as what they say.

Twilight Zone

What's Your Sign? 344

Subject: Just for Fun
Preparation: None

If you've ever looked to the stars to tell your future, here's a way to chart your own course.

Over dinner, review the horoscope page taken from your newspaper, and revise the traditional zodiac signs to suit your family. In our house, Aries, Taurus, Gemini, Aquarius, Leo, and Virgo have spawned Tyrannosaurus Rex, Pizza, Hotstuff, Floormop, Shampoo, and Crouton.

Now take a day and have somebody predict the course for the day. For example, a friend of ours has the sign T-Rex, and his horoscope is Pizza is passing through Hotstuff today, which presents a perfect opportunity to renew old friendships with dinosaurs. Watch out for loose boulders and unevolved cavepeople.

You may become a successful fortune-teller. Anyway, we predict that you'll have some fun!

Gazette Games

Subject: Geography

Preparation: None

S ometimes children need help to grasp the concept of different time zones—that people who live far away may just be waking up when we're getting ready to go to sleep, for instance. Here's an activity that is sure to help children imagine how time zones work.

During this dinnertime activity, each family member first chooses a different time zone to live in (Eastern Standard Time, Central Time, and so on). Then have each person discuss what he or she is doing right now. If it's dinnertime in Boston, what might somebody be doing in California? How about in Arizona? Now, change the time. Say that you're just waking up. Again, have everybody at the table say what he or she is doing.

Another way to play the game with older kids is to choose different countries. Continue in the same way as before. While you're eating dinner, what is your child in Australia doing? The time will just fly when you're having fun!

Subject: Family Circle

Preparation: None

F airness is a tough issue for kids to grapple with. So why not pose this question at the dinner table—you might find the answers helpful the next time there are more wants and fewer choices to go around:

Lots of times family members want to do different things—one person might want to play outside and another might want to play inside. What's a fair way to decide what to do?

Fifty Questions

347 When I Was a Baby I . . .

Subject: Just for Fun
Preparation: Photocopy family pictures

Younger children love to hear about what they were like as babies, and older ones are sure to relish the thought of their own parents as tots!

After dinner, pass around some photocopies of baby pictures—preferably of everyone at the table, parents included. Then, have everyone pick out a photo—of someone other than him- or herself—and take turns "putting words in the mouth" of the subject of the picture. Older kids can draw a "balloon" and write in humorous comments offered by family members. For instance, a toddler walking on wobbly legs might be thinking, "What did we decide was wrong with crawling, anyway?"

Finally, pass the photos back to the person pictured and share any memories that the pictures bring to mind, jotting down the thoughts in your Family Album. Why was the picture taken—had somebody just bought a new camera that he or she wanted to try out, or was the baby just too cute to resist snapping?

Family Album

Where Are You Headed? 348

Subject: Geography
Preparation: None

A tricky skill for some children (and many parents) to acquire is a sense of direction. It's also a useful art—especially if you hope to see parts of the country that lie beyond your dinner table!

To start the game, choose a direction, then, have each family member name a place—a street, city, or state—that lies that way. You can continue until everyone runs out of answers. Change directions, and begin again.

Another way to play this game is to limit everybody's answers to places in only one category. For example, how many cities can you think of that lie to the south? You might even unfold a map or two to check your answers. (Sorry kids, but according to our map, Bangor, Maine does *not* lie to the south of Providence, Rhode Island!)

Game Time

349 Where the Heart Is

Subject: Neighborhood Awareness

Preparation: None

What's extra special about your home town? Find out with this table talk activity.

Over dinner, have family members describe your home and community as though they were speaking to somebody who had never been there before. What are the things about your home that are special and might induce an out-of-towner to move there?

Alternatively, try imagining your family as a tourist bureau for a place you've visited together. Who wouldn't want to see Fenway Park, Faneuil Hall, and the Old North Church in Boston? Or the Statue of Liberty, Radio City Music Hall, and the Empire State Building in New York? Have your family work as a travel guide team to "recommend" restaurants, shops, historical sites, and all the other must-see attractions.

Your family might even jumpstart the travel industry or create a new real estate boom!

---

350 Which Way Did It Go?

Subject: Health Matters

Preparation: None

People come in many different pack-ages—and with good reason, we're sure. (If everyone looked the same, how would we ever recognize our family and friends?) So how about trying to solve this appearance-related puzzle at the dinner table:

Fifty Questions

Why do some men lose their hair as they grow older . . . and why are some babies born with no hair at all?

Subject: History
Preparation: None

Here is a chance to portray some of your favorite personalities in history, with an added plus: you'll find out just what your family knows about some of these folks!

During or after dinner, choose one family member to be "it." It is up to that person to choose someone from history that he or she would like to portray. Older children can be encouraged to think of someone rather obscure, or a figure they learned about in school recently. For younger family members, subjects can even be drawn from their favorite fiction—like Winnie the Pooh or the Cat in the Hat. As for the portrayal itself, this can be a simple matter of thinking of the person, or it can be as developed as a full-fledged attempt at impersonation.

Once the figure is chosen, it is up to everyone else to try and guess his or her identity through questions. Is he or she an American? At what period in history was the person famous? Did the person in question change the progress of the world?

Good luck with your guesses!

Guessing Games

Subject: Careers and Occupations
Preparation: None

During the day, all of us encounter people doing a variety of jobs, from the meter reader and teacher to the salesperson and doctor. This dinner table "charades" activity will stimulate everyone at the table to take a closer look at what various occupations entail.

After dinner, one person begins by pantomiming a person on the job. Perhaps the mail carrier is slightly listing to one side because of the heavy mail sack. He or she holds a stack of letters and sorts it out before pushing it through the mail slot. He or she then adjusts the bag and walks down the "sidewalk" before repeating the same sequence at the next "house." Whoever guesses the correct answer does the next impersonation (make sure everyone gets a chance to be "on the job" before dinner is adjourned).

Of course, this activity can get quite esoteric—especially when your son or daughter impersonates a famous local poet he or she has just learned about in school!

Guessing Games

Subject: Arts and Media

Preparation: Make a ballot box

How would you like to bring the excitement of a movie awards ceremony to your dinner table? All you need is a family of enthusiastic cinema-goers, and opinionated "critics."

Have your family "academy" nominate candidates for various categories: best leading actor and actress, funniest animated character, most touching plot, neatest songs, most surprising (or satisfying) ending, coolest performance by a kid, bravest hero, and movie you'd most like to see again.

Of course, you should give the "turkeys" their due, too. Nominate your picks for: ending that you'd most like to rewrite, dullest storyline, and overall theatrical "dud," or perhaps the movie that had the most overblown buildup.

Then have the "judges" cast their votes by folding in half slips of paper with their choices and putting them in the ballot box. Have someone sort and count the votes, and then get ready to take turns announcing the results at the dinner table. The envelope, please!

Subject: Self and Emotions

Preparation: None

It's been said that we're never given a dream without also being given the power to make the dream come true. What about your family's hopes? Do some things seem unattainable? Ask your family this dinner table question:

What is an impossible thing that you wish could happen, and why?

Fifty Questions

355 Women Presidents

Subject: Politics
Preparation: None

Some people think that a woman's place is in the home . . . and in the Oval Office. One day a woman might be elected president of the United States. Do you hope the day arrives soon—or not at all?

It's Never Been Done

We've never had a woman president, and people (especially men) would be nervous if we elected one. Most women wouldn't want to be president anyway—they know that they're not really cut out for the job.

Running the Country

Women can do anything that men can do, and they probably can do most things even better than men. It's time to give women a chance.

Great Debates

Workday Awards 356

Subject: Careers and Occupations
Preparation: Make a ballot box

What do firefighters, mail clerks, teachers, taxi drivers, plumbers, doctors, and store clerks all have in common? Just try to last a couple of weeks without them!

Have your family elect "Workday Award" recipients. Start by nominating candidates: the most essential job in your community; the most exciting occupation; the most dangerous; the most difficult; the most underappreciated; the most glamorous; and the most rewarding. Have voters write down the category and their choices on slips of paper, then insert the papers in the dinner table ballot box. An "election worker" can sort them by categories and tabulate the votes.

Have all the people you encounter frequently in your community been recognized? You wouldn't want to leave anyone out—how would you feel if your pizza delivery person or ice cream truck driver chose this week to go on strike?

Cast Your Vote

Subject: Self and Emotions

Preparation: None

Great Thoughts

Wise words to ponder:

Necessity is the mother of invention.

Start a great dinner table discussion by asking:

1. Can you think of a time when you came up with a clever solution to a problem? What "pushed" you to do so?

2. Do you know about the history of any important inventions? What need did the invention fill?

3. Could we find solutions to all of the problems of the world if we just decided that we really needed to solve them?

Subject: Geography

Preparation: None

Family Book Works

There's a whole world to explore, and it's sitting right on your bookshelf. Flip to any page in an atlas (or spin a globe), and have somebody point to a country. Then, see whether he or she can answer some questions about it, such as: "What language do people there speak?" . . . "What is the climate like?" . . . "What kind of food do the people eat?" . . . "Are there any unusual animals, natural wonders?" And so on.

You can scale the activity for children of all ages; even a young child can play—you might be surprised to know that the main staple of the Republic of Vermont is chocolate, and that it is the only part of the world where the sun never sets (hence there's no need for children to go to sleep!).

As a variation, have one person select a place for the rest of the family. The family members can then take turns answering questions about the selected place. Who knows what hidden knowledge your family will unearth as the globe turns!

Subject: Just for Fun
Preparation: None

Let's say that you and your family were magically endowed with the ability to see the future. You knew what everyone was going to say before he or she said it, and you knew what was going to happen that day before you even got out of bed.

Have your family take turns answering the following questions: What would you most want to know about your own future? How would you use the information to make your life better? What would you want to know about the future of the world? How would you use that information to help people? How would you convince the authorities that you could, indeed, see the future?

Also, would you use your fortune telling abilities to make money? How? Would you tell people more about the future than they wanted to know? Why or why not? What other challenges and temptations would you face as a teller of the future?

Onward!

Twilight Zone

Subject: Books and Literature
Preparation: None

It doesn't always take inspiration to be a poet. Sometimes a collection of good books and pictures is all that's required!

After dinner, excuse each person from the table for a moment to round up his or her favorite illustrated book—perhaps it's a book of drawings or paintings, or perhaps it's a favorite illustrated story. Then, one at a time, take turns sharing your favorite picture with the rest of the family. With each picture, try your hand at composing a poem that does the image justice. (Remember, not all poetry rhymes. Have you written a haiku poem lately?) If you prefer, you can appoint a scribe to do the writing, or use a tape recorder instead.

Your scribe might want to copy your family's poems into a homemade "blank book." They're sure to bring back fond memories—of both family dinners *and* literature—in years to come.

Family Book Works

361 The Year 2494

Subject: Role Play
Preparation: None

The date: 2494 A.D. The place: your house. The event: mealtime.

Have your family act out what life will be like about 500 years in the future. What kinds of jobs do people have? And what kinds of jobs do people have? How do they travel? And what does the family do together for fun?

Now, try going back in time to 2494 B.C. Answer the same questions, and add the following: What wild animals present the biggest dangers? How does your family stay warm in the winter and keep cool in the summer? What kinds of things do they do for themselves that people in our time don't?

After your family has improvised a day in the life in the years 2494 A.D. and B.C., have them compare the years to each other, and then to the present. You might discover the age-old truth: Now is the best time of your life!

Dinner Theater

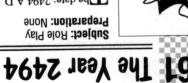

362 Young and Old

Subject: Self and Emotions
Preparation: None

We usually think of teachers as being older than their students. But can kids be teachers, too? This question is sure to evoke some surprising answers. Ask:

What can grownups learn from kids?

Fifty Questions

Subject: Science and Nature
Preparation: None

Even the smallest "postage stamp" backyard is teeming with interesting life. How many critters reside in or visit your yard during the course of the year? Find out with this table talk activity (which is especially good for younger kids).

During or after dinner, poll your family members about the ecology of your back yard. Have each member think about all the critters they have ever seen, great or small. Don't forget about insects and spiders, dogs and cats that visit from down the street, occasional visiting skunks or raccoons, and birds (migrating birds count too, since they pass through your "air space"). And don't forget the life

forms that live underground that you don't see until you disrupt their environment, such as earthworms, centipedes, grubs, and other "unhuggables."

Wait a minute. How about that two-legged creature you saw standing by the back steps just this morning? That's right, make sure no one forgets to add people to your list!

Play School

Subject: Friendship
Preparation: None

When's the last time you invited family friends and relatives to a special family event? Over dinner, get the family involved in planning the get-together.

Decide when the event will be held and whether it's to be a family Sunday brunch, a backyard barbecue, or a birthday celebration. Then, have everyone help put together the guest list—that way you're sure to include someone special for each family member. (Cross-check your list against your address books to make sure that you haven't accidentally missed anyone.) Have your family brainstorm to develop party activities, foods, decorations, favors, and invitations, while the family scribe writes down the ideas.

In the event that you don't have a conventional reason to have a party, you can still come up with a theme for your gathering. Any excuse will do—a potluck dinner, costume party, or puppet show. Later, with a little imagination, you can turn your dinner table plan into an event to remember!

What's the Plan

365 You're in Business

Subject: Just for Fun

Preparation: Clip ads and coupons

Does your family have what it takes to
be store owners? Pretend that you're
about to open a new business and you're
going on a shopping spree (choose pictures you've clipped from catalogs, old
magazines, or coupons) to stock your
shelves. Naturally you want to buy what
you need at the best possible prices so that
you can sell your goods at a reasonable cost.

Perhaps you've decided to open a supermarket.
See whether you can find pictures of the freshest
and most nutritious foods to entice customers. Remember to include products in all categories—dairy, meats,
breads, cereals, snacks, fruits, vegetables, etc. You wouldn't
want to lose business because you forgot to stock the makings
of a salad!

Or maybe you'd rather open a clothing store. You'll have to
find outstanding examples of men's, women's, and children's
latest fashions to put in the window.

So, who says that it's difficult to start a new business? You've
proven that you have what it takes to be an entrepreneur!

Playalong Junk
Mail

Activity Category Index

Activity Category Index (cont.)

Subject Index

Law and Justice

Money Matters

Neighborhood Awareness

Activities That Can Be Adapted for Younger Kids

Table Talk! Activity Log

#	ACTIVITY	DATE	COMMENT

About the Authors

Steve and Ruth Bennett's *365 TV-Free Activities You Can Do With Your Child* (Bob Adams, 1991) is a national bestseller. Their *365 Outdoor Activities You Can Do With Your Child* (Bob Adams, 1993) has also been well received. The couple also compiled *Kids' Answers to Life's Big Questions* (Bob Adams, 1992), which consists of responses to a nationwide survey of four-, five-, and six-year-olds, as well as original color artwork submitted by the children.

Steve Bennett is a full-time author who has written more than 40 books on business and the environment, entrepreneurship, management, and business computing. He holds a master's degree in Regional Studies from Harvard University, where he studied the ancient Chinese art of house and tomb placement.

Ruth Loetterle Bennett is a landscape architect and illustrator. She has designed parks, playgrounds, and other public places in a number of cities in the United States.

Ruth and Steve table talk with their two children, Audrey and Noah, in Cambridge, Massachusetts.

Do you have any great *Table Talk!* activities that are favorites in your family? If you'd like to share them with us, please write:

Steve and Ruth Bennett
P.O. Box 1090
Cambridge, MA 02238

If we use your idea(s) in future editions, we'll be sure to give you credit in the book, along with a free copy.

(All entries become the sole property of Steve and Ruth Bennett.)